P9-ECO-336

HOOKED ON CUSTOMERS

The Five Habits of Legendary Customer-Centric Companies

Robert G. Thompson

customer
THINK

2014

Hooked On Customers

Copyright © 2014 Robert G. Thompson. All rights reserved

Published by CustomerThink Corp.

www.customerthink.com

Without limiting the rights under copyright reserved above, no part of this publication
may be reproduced, stored in or introduced into a database and retrieval system
or transmitted in any form or any means (electronic, mechanical, photocopying,
recording or otherwise) without the prior written permission of both the owner of
copyright and the above publishers. Requests for permission should be directed to
permissions@customerthink.com.

First Printing: April 2014
ISBN: 1478271515
ISBN 9781478271512

Praise for *Hooked On Customers*

"Bob Thompson draws on decades of his experience and research, as well as the insights of thought leaders in the field of customer-driven business strategy, to distill timeless principles for winning the minds and hearts of buyers—and growing profits. The book is full of data, examples, and case studies spotlighting innovative practices that you can use immediately."

—William Band, vice-president and principal analyst for Forrester Research, Inc.

"*Hooked on Customers* is a remarkable book, inspired by genius! Bob Thompson has packed powerful prose backed by solid research in a book that reads like a novel, not a textbook. Chock-full of solid advice illustrated by poignant examples, he has put his pen on the pulse of how great leaders create, nurture, and sustain organizations renowned for growth-producing customer-centric practices. If you care about your customers, don't miss this great book."

—Chip R. Bell, author of *The 9 ½ Principles of Innovative Service*

"Bob Thompson has written an outstanding guide for those people and organizations truly committed to being customer-centric and creating great customer experiences. It is the most comprehensive study I've seen, packed with stories, data, and pragmatic advice to help you build and execute your strategy to be a customer-centric business. Thompson has filled his book with examples and data to help you better understand what "best in class" organizations do and the results that can be produced. Don't just read it, use it as a working guide to help you develop and execute your plan to create a business that focuses on its customers and drives great customer loyalty."

—Dave Brock, founder of Partners In EXCELLENCE

"Once you decide that a customer-centric culture is the only path to sustainable differentiation in your business, you need this book to outline your path forward. Bob Thompson is the go-to guy on customer strategies. His common sense and practical ideas will leave you wishing you had had this book years ago."

—Greg Gianforte, founder of RightNow, coauthor of *Attack of the Customers*

"Very few people have Bob Thompson's vast experience and understanding of the tools and strategies for customer-centric business, combined with an instinct for business success. Together, the knowledge creates an outstanding resource. In this book, Thompson generously shares his most practical and useful advice to inspire customer-centric leaders to emerge and energetically drive success for their businesses."

—Pat Gibbons, senior vice-president of marketing for Walker

"When it comes to customer-based business strategies, Bob Thompson is one of the deepest thinkers I know. He ceaselessly looks for new insights, for proven strategies, for missing answers, and for new ways to learn. In this book, Thompson has crammed two decades of experience to tell you precisely what to *never* do and then explains what you should *always* do. It's a true gem."

—Bruce Kasanoff, founder of Now Possible, coauthor of *Smart Customers, Stupid Companies*

"This is a must-read for practitioners and anyone involved in managing and capturing the voice of the customer. Bob Thompson puts the issues and challenges in context, then rightfully acknowledges and pushes beyond the subject of strategy with a relentless focus on execution and implementation. Honing in on the practical 'hows' and 'whats,' this is a book about doing. After this, Thompson may have to change the name of his company from CustomerThink to CustomerAction."

—Howard Lax, senior vice-president for GfK Custom Research North America

"Three words describe Bob Thompson's approach to customer-first business: sound, sound, sound. Throughout all the years I've known him, he has never gone for the latest sound bite or slogan. Everything Thompson says and writes is thoughtful and well considered. Plus, I know no one more knowledgeable in this field. He's a trusty guide and writes well to boot!"

—Dick Lee, founder of High-Yield Methods, author of *The Customer Relationship Survival Guide*

"Comprehensive and concise! After reading the book, I have a feeling that I'd grasped the most important elements out of the topics of CRM and CEM. Thompson wrote it in a way that it's so easy to read, understand, and remember, integrating human factors and technologies. 'Food for thought' will stimulate readers to think of their own situations."

—Sampson Lee, founder of Global CEM Organization

"*Hooked on Customers* reveals the secret to running a customer-centric business. It's not what you say but rather what you do. Great companies forge a culture of "doing" that engrains five habits: listen, think, empower, create, and delight. Bob Thompson pulls back the curtain, showing how each of these behaviors interrelates to create the overall customer experience. The book is a must-read for any leader who wants to win the hearts of their employees and customers."

—Stan Phelps, founder of 9 Inch Marketing, author of *What's Your Purple Goldfish?*

"When I've read definitions of customer-centricity, they've been across the map, from 'It's a culture' to 'It's a process' to 'It's really a way of thinking.' Although these perspectives are helpful, the range of opinion points to a challenge: making customer-centricity pragmatic in a business strategy is about as easy as picking up a raw egg with a fork. *Hooked on Customers* offers excellent thought on this challenging topic and provides useful definitions and real-world examples in an organized, easy-to-follow outline. Most important, Bob Thompson's book asks and answers some vexing questions about customer-centricity, absent the cliché hype that we often see written on the topic."

—Andrew Rudin, managing principal for Outside Technologies, Inc.

"Bob Thompson has been at the epicenter of the customer movement for over ten years. He has his finger on the pulse of the latest trends and is connected with many of the leading authors around the world. No wonder then his new book is a treasure trove of insights, references, and tips. His five-step model is deceptively simple but contains a great deal of best practice gleaned over the years. If you are in any way interested in customer-centricity, this will be a welcome addition to your bookshelf."

—Shaun Smith, coauthor of *Bold: How to Be Brave in Business and Win*

"*Hooked on Customers* can be found at the crossroads of "the customer is always right" and "data-driven business." It is decidedly *not* a flag-waving cheerleader for some new buzzword management practice but a sound review of the latest case studies and technical advances to help you understand the value of creating a better customer experience as a path to profitability. This is the book that can help you change your corporate culture to the delight of your customers."

—Jim Sterne, founder of Target Marketing of Santa Barbara, author of *Social Media Metrics*

"Bob Thompson asks questions that make you think, but also, that make you want to *act*. To stop doing what you've always done and start doing what you need to do. In *Hooked on Customers*, each chapter outlines important parts of a customer-centric orientation; each ends with questions that, when you can answer directly, will take you well down the path to success.

—Barry Trailer, managing partner of CSO Insights and author of *Sales Mastery*

For Regina

Contents

Foreword xiii

Preface xvii

Introduction 1

    Strategy Is Overrated 2

    Customer-centric Business Management 6

    What You Will Learn in This Book 9

A Brief History 13

    Why Did CRM Fail to Drive Loyalty? 14

    What Are We Managing? 16

    Customer Experience Management 18

    Managing the Yin and Yang of Customer Relationships 22

Habit 1—Listen 23

    Measure Twice, Cut Once. What Really Drives Loyalty? 24

    The Ultimate Loyalty Metric for Your Business 32

    The Voice of Customer Command Center 36

    Closing the Loop with Social Customers 44

Habit 2—Think 49

    Oh, the Thinks That We Think 50

    Using Analytics to Improve the Consumer Experience 56

    Mining Unstructured Text to Find Golden Nuggets 63

Use Speech Analytics to Reduce Frustrating Calls............................ 66

Harmonize the Cross-Channel Service Experience 69

Habit 3—Empower... 74

The Employee Engagement "Leap of Faith" 75

Improve Your AIM to Empower Service Reps............................... 81

Is Social Software the Cure for Business as Usual? 88

Work Backward from the Customer 95

Lean, Not Mean. Southwest's Key to Profitable Growth.............. 101

Habit 4—Create 107

Creativity, Invention, and Innovation 108

Delight, by Design. Innovation Sets Intuit Apart...................... 113

How Weber and Home Depot Earned My Business 118

Shopper Psychology: Why CEO Ron Johnson

Failed at JC Penney 121

How Amazon Wins: Innovation, Low Prices,

and Free Cash Flow 127

Habit 5—Delight 130

Keep Trying to Delight Your Customers 131

People: The Secret Sauce in Delightful Experiences...................... 137

If the Customer Experience Is So Important,

How Do You Explain the Success of Ryanair?.......................... 145

Three Roles for Technology in Customer Delight 148

Leadership 155

Worst to First: Sprint's Dramatic Turnaround.......................... 156

Do You Need a Chief Customer Officer?................................. 166

Customer-centric Maturity Stages.. 169

Afterword 175

Acknowledgments... 179

Notes... 183

About the Author.. 203

Foreword

Is customer-centricity "real" or "Memorex"? Can it be regained inside an organization that once grew because of its commitment to customers and employees? Can it be breathed into one that has never known it?

Yes. But it takes gut and guts.

You need to know what kind of leader you're working with as you contemplate taking on this work. And sometimes it is just plain hard to get past the great language and know if the commitment is real. Bob Thompson gives you the secret decoder ring in this book to help you investigate what type of leader you're considering working with or committing to. Knowing the difference will make the difference…between success and mediocrity in the transformation you're considering taking on in your business.

For twenty-five years inside five great US companies, I had the fifty-ton weight of "just go fix it" strapped to my back regarding driving customer-centricity—making customers as the asset of the business the core of the company's growth strategy. I've worked with enlightened leaders where we've been in lockstep every step of the way. Having had the good fortune to begin my customer zealotry career at Lands' End, reporting to founder Gary Comer, I received the foundation to know when that path was right. But I've spent way too much time pounding on doors to get into meetings and onto the agenda and to have a seat in the room where the big decisions are made.

Here's what I know for sure. This work won't budge from hand wave to action without two leadership attributes: gut and guts.

Gut. *Gut* leaders know the higher purpose they want to have for their customers. They have sharpened radar for seeing what's right and wrong and what's getting in the way. They've got an internal compass and instinct for how to get there. And they have a clear line of sight for where they want to take the company.

Guts. Leaders with *guts* will absolutely take the hill to get there. They will make the customer agenda a priority of the organization. There will be no settling for mediocrity. They've got the chops to stick their neck out and will do it to make things happen. They will push the company and push back on the company until they get it right. Customer priority and issues will be known, understood, and thought about at all levels, straight up to the board.

In this book, Thompson builds upon what I penned as "gut" and "guts" leadership in my book *Chief Customer Officer: Getting Past Lip Service to Passionate Action*, to translate them for you into five behaviors. Use this information to look under the hood—to know and understand the leaders you are working for or considering working for. Use his book as a guide to fashion the behaviors in yourself to build the customer-focused leaders you aspire for your organization.

You know, love is irrational. *Customer love* comes from what some consider irrational business behavior and leadership habits. Companies that grow get a disproportionate piece of the pie because their leaders are not always looking over their shoulder at what each decision will get them.

But that takes gut and guts. And embedding Thompson's habits into how you lead your business life.

Jeanne Bliss
Los Angeles, California

Jeanne Bliss is founder of CustomerBLISS, author of *Chief Customer Officer: Getting Past Lip Service to Passionate Action,* and cofounder of the Customer Experience Professionals Association.

Preface

This book is the result of fifteen years of research, collaboration, and thinking about what makes customer-centric firms tick. The foundation for much of this work is the online community I launched in 2000 as CRMGuru.com and renamed in 2007 to CustomerThink.com.

However, IBM deserves credit for fundamentals that would eventually get turned into terms like Customer Relationship Management (CRM), Customer Experience Management (CEM), and Voice of Customer. In 1978 I joined IBM straight out of college after earning a bachelor's degree in mathematics and an MBA. My first year was spent in training, where I learned the three basic beliefs: 1) respect for the individual, 2) best possible customer service, and 3) pursuit of excellence. These beliefs were part of the company's culture and became part of mine, too.

My most memorable experience came early in my career, just a couple of years out of training, while working as a systems engineer with one of IBM's big grocery customers. In a status meeting, I complained passionately about my customer's lack of action on an important project—one that I thought was in their best interest. After my outburst the CIO pulled me aside and expressed his displeasure. When I said he misunderstood me and that my intentions were good, he just replied: "Perception is reality." As you read on, you'll learn why this is such a critical insight. Understanding customer *perceptions* is a core behavior of customer-centric leaders.

After my career at IBM, I spent three years running a UNIX systems reseller. In 1998, wanting to shift to professional services and thought leadership, I hung up a shingle as a CRM consultant. Why? Because CRM seemed like a wonderful blend of business strategy, customer-centric thinking, and technology.

My first few years were spent specializing in Partner Relationship Management (PRM), an emerging niche focused on channel partner relationships. I still found time to start a general CRM email newsletter in 1998 followed by email-based discussion list (CRM.Talk) in 1999. Both grew rapidly but remained hobbies that I supported as a sideline to my day job as a PRM consultant and industry analyst.

That started to change in 2000 when I launched CRMGuru.com, initially just to archive email newsletters and discussions. But I also wanted to provide a service to help answer questions because it was clear that many people were confused about CRM. Experts in different customer-related specialties joined me to volunteer time to answer questions as "CRM.Talk Gurus."

CRMGuru.com took off immediately and our email newsletter list grew to be the largest in the industry. By 2003 my business shifted to CRM research and publishing. During the first half of the decade, we were fortunate to have many more top industry experts from around the world shape the community's direction and share their insights via articles and discussions. (See the acknowledgments for more about our top contributors.)

The CRM boom didn't last. CRM was widely described as a failure in media reports. By 2005 it became apparent that CRM was falling far short of my vision at the beginning. Sadly most people thought of CRM as a way to automate marketing, sales, and service processes, not as a loyalty-building strategy.

Fortunately a new idea was pushing forward as a counterbalance to CRM's inside-out technology obsession: Customer Experience Management (CEM). After a major CEM research study and a lot of soul searching, in 2007 I changed the community's name from CRMGuru to CustomerThink. At the time it was a controversial move, but I believed that a more neutral name—not built around an industry acronym—would help us cover CEM and other new developments over the long term. And indeed it has. That year we also upgraded our website to enable authors to blog. Along with our name change, the stage was set for a rapid increase in contributed content and visitors in the years that followed.

As this book goes to press, CustomerThink.com has over fifteen hundred contributing authors! Collectively they submit over seven thousand blog posts and articles per year, covering all facets of customer-centric business, including CRM, CEM, social business, analytics, and innovation. Annually CustomerThink.com serves about one million visitors from two hundred countries around the world, from Afghanistan to Zimbabwe.

In my fifteen years in this "customer relationship" industry, I've traveled the globe speaking at conferences to evangelize customer-centric strategy and best practices. I've been blessed to know many of the brightest minds in the industry. I've learned that there is no one way to succeed. Depending on a company's market position and capabilities, there are many paths to move forward. I've observed that every methodology has its place, but none works everywhere.

I wrote this book to share what I've learned and shorten your learning curve. However, if you are looking for a "magic" metric or five easy steps that will guarantee your success, this book is not for you.

That said, if you read this book, then put it down and do nothing, I'll be very disappointed. My bigger goal is to stimulate your *action*. At the conclusion of each chapter you'll find "food for thought." Take these questions to your leaders, peers, and employees for a candid discussion about your organization's strengths, weaknesses, and opportunities for improvement. Then build a plan to *do* something.

It takes a lot to create a customer-centric success story. Leaders who envision the future and inspire others. Strategists who think and plan. Supporters who put the new ideas to work. Techies who evangelize and implement new tools. And, yes, even critics who question conventional wisdom.

Are you ready to move forward on your customer-centric journey? Then read on and get started!

Introduction

We have a strategic plan. It's called doing things.
—Herb Kelleher

Over the years, I've heard many times that "[insert breaking trend here] is a strategy" to compete, grow, differentiate, etc. I must confess that I said the same thing myself back in the early days of the CRM industry.

Let me get this straight. CRM is a strategy. CEM is a strategy. Social media is a strategy. Analytics is a strategy. Oh, and let's not leave out my personal favorite: customer-centricity is a strategy, too.

What's left? Everything is a strategy!

"Strategy" used in this way is meaningless puffery to make something seem more important. But strategy should mean something if you use it in the context of a specific business—*your* business.

What strategy should be is a long-term, high-level plan to accomplish important business goals—like profitable growth and increasing shareholder value. A strategy should include major decisions, such as which markets to serve and how to win business and build loyal customer relationships within those markets.

Tactics, on the other hand, are all about execution—getting the plan done.

Looking at popular trends this way, are they really strategies for any specific company to win? How can it possibly be true that your company will get a competitive advantage with sales automation, customer experience, social media, or analytics when these same "strategies" are available and used by everyone?

In my view, none of these qualify as business strategies, and neither does the fuzzy notion of customer-centricity. They are useful ideas, methods, and tools that you can use to *support* a real business strategy for your organization. But they can't generically do anything for your company.

Strategy Is Overrated

Let me be clear that I do believe it's critical to have a real business strategy for differentiation. Be it on product excellence, customer experience, cost, convenience, or whatever—every business should have a plan to focus its resources to maximize success.

Although such strategies are critical, they don't change frequently. Look at industry leaders and you'll find they don't lurch from one strategy to the next every year. Southwest Airlines has followed its low-cost business strategy for more than four decades. Apple has been hell-bent on making "insanely great" products with Steve Jobs at the helm.

Of course, you might argue, and I would agree, that the business world is littered with examples of companies that did not make good strategic choices or waited too long in doing so. Poor strategic choices may explain why Best Buy succeeded and Circuit City failed. Or why Motorola and Nokia, among others, missed the shift to modern smartphones, while Apple and Samsung have prospered.

But these shifts in strategy, while critical, are not what this book is about. Rather, it's about *executing your current business strategy better by getting closer to your customers.*

Is Customer Experience Really a Strategy?

Since everyone seems to be hopping on the customer experience strategy bandwagon now, let me use that to illustrate my point. First, let's remember that every company delivers a customer experience (CX) whether it's done intentionally or not. Can something be a strategy when it's a normal outcome of conducting any business?

Second, studies by Forrester Research found that about nine out of ten executives say they want to *differentiate* based on CX. Ah, differentiation sounds strategic, doesn't it? Here's the problem: How are 90 percent of companies going to be different by using the same strategy as everyone else?

Of course, that's not what I'd say if I were leading one of those companies. I would say that I intend to do a better job of providing a differentiated CX by providing *more responsive customer service*, supporting *new digital channels*, hiring and *training clerks* in my store—or whatever made my customers happier to do business with me and not my competitors.

All of this, of course, is still not a unique strategy because my competitors are doing the same thing. Or at least their proclaimed strategies would lead you to believe they are trying.

Still don't believe me? Forrester Research predicted in 2012 that "C-level execs [would] officially name customer experience a top strategic priority." The analyst firm cites an IBM 2012 study where CEOs named "customer obsession" as the top leadership trait required to steer their organizations effectively, and 66 percent listed "customer relationships" as a key source of sustained economic value. Furthermore, 73 percent said that they're investing heavily in "customer insights."[1]

Wow, it's great that all things customer are coming to the top of CEO agendas. But it also means that many, if not most, firms in an industry will try to do essentially the same thing: obsess about customers, build loyal relationships, and leverage customer insight. Strategic advantage: none.

A Culture of Execution

The hard truth is the vast majority of companies that win don't have a unique strategy—quite the opposite. They are doing what everyone else is doing but have figured out how to execute better. Yes, there are exceptions, but we can't all emulate Apple. And Zappos, the oft-quoted example of service excellence, is not at all unique in its strategy, just the fanatical way it executes against a strategy of "delivering happiness."

That's why I've come to the conclusion that "strategy" is an abused term and overrated as the key to business success in general and customer-centric success in particular. *Execution is what separates the winners and losers.*

Let's take one of my favorite airlines, Southwest, to illustrate. The company's strategy of delivering affordable, dependable, and friendly air travel has resulted in four decades of profitability in an industry that is perpetually drowning in red ink. Is low-cost air travel a unique idea? Of course not. Many airlines have tried and failed to duplicate Southwest's success. Kelleher found that the secret was not the strategy itself but rather execution. Oh, and Southwest didn't invent the strategy either. Founder Herb Kelleher based the business model on ideas gleaned from Pacific Southwest Airlines.[2]

Even former GE chairperson and famed business strategist Jack Welch said: "In real life, strategy is actually very straightforward. You pick a general direction and execute like hell."

If your game plan is to be the low-cost provider in your industry, customer-centricity can help you improve performance against that strategy. If you intend to differentiate based on a highly engaging customer experience, the five habits discussed in this book will improve your ability to deliver that brand promise. If you aspire to be the "Apple" of your industry, customer-centric innovation will increase your ability to create new value for customers and your business.

> The hard truth is the vast majority of companies that win don't have a unique strategy—quite the opposite.

Let me reiterate that business strategy is incredibly important. Ideally companies should have a sound business strategy backed by solid execution. (Read the last chapter on customer-centric leadership to learn how Sprint's strategy shift backed up with solid customer-centric execution helped bring the firm back from the brink.) Still, once a direction is set by top management regarding the markets to serve and product/services to sell to those markets, success is largely a function of execution. That is the focus of this book.

The Business Case for Customer-centricity

What's the point of being customer-centric? *Customers of leading customer-centric companies are more genuinely loyal, which drives long-term profitable growth and shareholder value.* By "genuinely" I mean loyal in both purchasing *behavior* (retention) and advocacy *attitude* (positive feeling).

Loyal customers drive business value as they:

- Continue to do business (it is usually less costly to retain customers than to acquire new customers)

- Increase purchases over time (customers are more receptive to increasing spend and buying new products/services)

- Share positive views about a company and its solutions (essentially free marketing, as customers influence others through word of mouth)

If you aspire to be a customer-centric firm, you *must* learn how to measure your customers' loyalty and understand how it links to your business performance. (See the "Listen" chapter for details on loyalty drivers.) For a macro cross-industry view, however, consider the robust methodology used in The American Customer Satisfaction Index (ACSI), developed by Claes Fornell in conjunction with the National Quality Research Center (NQRC), Stephen M. Ross School of Business at the University of Michigan. ACSI measures consumer satisfaction with goods and services in the United States. Fornell's research has found that ACSI is *predictive* of corporate performance, growth in the Gross Domestic Product (GDP), and changes in consumer spending.[3]

This is critical because most methodologies claim a simple correlation as justification for validity. (See the "Think" chapter for more on confusing correlation with causation.) Fornell and his collaborators found that ACSI predicts shareholder value. A portfolio of stocks chosen based on high ACSI scores dramatically outperformed the S&P 500. Investing $100 in the ACSI fund from April 2000 to April 2012 yielded $490, a gain of 390 percent. During that same period, the S&P 500 returned only $93, a 7 percent loss.[4]

Customer-centric Business Management

Customer-centricity is not a goal; it's a management approach to executing a business strategy. I define Customer-centric Business Management (CBM) simply as:

Delivering the total customer value that drives genuinely loyal customer attitudes and behaviors in a target market.

The point of CBM is to drive superior execution of the company's business strategy, resulting in competitive differentiation and long-term profitable growth for the enterprise. CBM is about translating the aspiration of being a leading customer-centric firm into business results.

The key phrases in this definition are:

- **Total customer value:** What customers *perceive* as valuable

- **Genuinely loyal:** Not just retention, but also an emotional bond

- **Target market:** The market in which you intend to do business

Definitions are easy. Accomplishing what I've described is an entirely different matter. It requires a systemic approach to running a business where five customer-centric behaviors become engrained habits.

A System of Behaviors

Habits are routine organizational behaviors that work together as a system. Improving one part of a system without understanding how it relates to others would be like "putting a Rolls-Royce engine in a Hyundai" according to Russell Ackoff, an outspoken advocate of "systemic" thinking. He criticizes, as do I, the tendency of managers to analyze individual parts of a system but fail to understand how *the system as a whole* performs.

Most managers currently manage the actions of their organizations' parts taken separately. This is based on the false assumption that improving the performance of the parts separately necessarily improves the performance of the whole, the corporation. That is a false premise. In fact, you can destroy a corporation by improving its individual parts.[5]

For example, marketing, sales, and support organizations often have a tense relationship with each other, especially in business-to-business companies. Marketing is rewarded for building a brand and generating leads, while sales is the hero for closing deals. Customer service is viewed as a cost center, getting no credit for closed sales and revenue growth, only blame when customers complain or defect.

With business leaders working independently—each responsible for their departmental "silos" with unique measurements and rewards—it is hardly surprising that teamwork is a challenge. One common problem is marketing generating a high volume of leads that sales promptly throws away as "low quality," meaning not immediately ready to buy. Another is customer service cutting costs at the behest of the CFO without any concern for customer defections, which makes the job of marketing more expensive as it tries to fill the "leaky bucket."

Take a step back and ask yourself: What is the goal of the *entire* organization? Optimizing profitable growth is probably at the top of your CEO's agenda, and yet improving one part of a marketing-sales-support "system" may actually undermine that goal.

As Ackoff observed, optimizing the parts of a system doesn't necessarily optimize the overall results. And yet, ROI studies abound to "prove" that investing in a new tool or methodology will improve one part of the system. You can't blame managers for grasping at such solutions if they have no vested interest in the bigger picture—such as customer loyalty, revenue growth, or another objective that spans organization silos.

Strong leadership is required to break through this "upgrade the parts" thinking. Consider Enterasys, a fast-growing global provider of enterprise networking solutions. According to Ram Appalaraju, senior VP of worldwide marketing, taking an end-to-end approach to revenue performance has enabled the firm to get better visibility of future business, optimize investments in marketing campaigns, and "significantly" improve staff productivity—all critical business issues that will help the company attain ambitious business goals.

However, Appalaraju is not just concerned with optimizing marketing and sales processes. If you think about revenue productivity holistically, you should consider the complete prospect/customer experience. Customer service/support is also a factor in loyal relationships, which helps drive revenue from existing customers.[6]

Makes sense, but when was the last time you heard a customer service agent getting credit when a sales rep booked a repeat order?

What You Will Learn in This Book

In *The Age of Discontinuity*, Peter Drucker wrote: "Lack of creativity is… not the problem of organization. Rather it is organizational inertia which always pushes for continuing what we are already doing."

What I've learned in my research is that the secret to success is not to fight organization inertia. Instead, make inertia your friend by embedding customer-centric habits in your company's culture. This book is about the five habits—routine behaviors that we repeat, usually without thinking or consciously deciding—of successful customer-centric companies.

This book leads off with a brief history of customer-centricity to give you a context for how I've developed the five habits. In a summary of key developments over the past fifteen years, you'll learn how CRM and CEM relate to each other and why customer-centricity is an evolution, not a destination.

The next five chapters cover each of the habits in detail, including research, examples, and "food for thought" to help you take action.

- **Listen**—Understand What Customers Value; Act on Their Feedback

- **Think**—Make Smart, Fact-Based Decisions

- **Empower**—Give Employees Resources and Authority to Serve Customers

- **Create**—Produce New Value for Customers and the Company

- **Delight**—Exceed Expectations; Be Remarkable!

Finally, the closing chapter on customer-centric leadership includes a case study of how Sprint integrated the five habits to support its impressive turnaround. You'll also get thoughts on the key roles of the chief executive and chief customer officers in leading a customer-centric journey.

The Five Habits Are a System

Each of the five habits can individually add value to customer-centric businesses and can rightly claim to be a factor in the success of practitioners. In fact, in my research I find each is positively correlated with business success, measured by profitable revenue growth and competitive position. But none of them *uniquely* explains why some companies consistently outperform their competitors.

THE FIVE CUSTOMER-CENTRIC HABITS

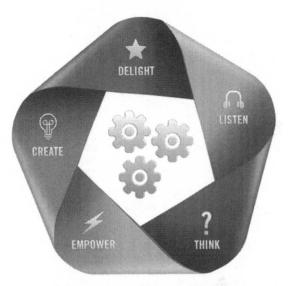

© Copyright 2014 CustomerThink Corp.

As you can see in my diagram, there is a logical flow to the habits. Listening is an input to thinking. Analysis can help you make better decisions on employee roles and which innovations will create the most value for customers. Creating new products and services is one source of customer delight.

But you should not assume this is a simple, step-by-step progression. The habits are *interrelated*, not linear. Analyzing customer loyalty drivers can also influence how to listen and collect feedback. While empowering employees may help delight customers, delightful experiences also create a more enjoyable work environment, which boosts employee productivity.

The five habits work together as a *systemic* approach to make customer-centricity a part of how business is done, day in and day out. This is what *culture* really means.

In a business context, I see culture as not just some ethereal notion of values and beliefs (yes, they do matter) but rather a set of behaviors. As some have put it more colorfully: "Culture is how we do things around here." Setting up the proper measurement and reward systems—depicted by the gears in the center of my diagram—is critical to reinforce the behaviors you seek. That's a key role for the CEO and other business leaders responsible for leading customer-centric efforts.

There's a tremendous opportunity to join legendary companies that lead customer satisfaction/loyalty ratings, like Amazon.com, Intuit, Southwest Airlines, and USAA. Are you ready to take your organization forward?

A Brief History

The purpose of a business is to create a customer.
—Peter Drucker

At a 2012 conference, I had an intriguing discussion with an executive for a large nonprofit organization hired to lead the organization's CRM activities. Shortly after starting she changed her job title to include "customer experience."

I asked her why. She replied that because of the "CRM" title, her boss expected that one of the first things to be decided was which CRM system to implement. The "customer experience" title, by contrast, allowed her to focus the organization on learning how constituents perceived their experiences—like giving donations, interacting with people, and web visits.

That process took a *year*. The CRM system had to wait.

Instead of choosing a system to automate what they were already doing, the nonprofit drove systems changes with an "outside-in" approach. Under the executive's leadership, they started by defining how their constituents' experience should look and feel to earn their loyalty. Then, and only then, they decided which systems were required to help support those experiences.

In just a few minutes, this story captured the essence of the debate that's been raging for years. Some CRM proponents say that it's all about customer loyalty, and delivering a great customer experience—the goal of Customer Experience Management (CEM)—is just part of that. Why, then, did this leader feel compelled to change her title?

Why Did CRM Fail to Drive Loyalty?

In CRM's heyday customer loyalty was one of the big benefits everyone talked about. Why didn't it work out that way? Speaking for all customers, I believe it boils down to three reasons:

1. *I am not a lead; I'm a person.* There are dozens of marketing automation systems designed to separate the wheat (qualified leads) from the chaff (time-wasting prospects). While it's true that marketing organizations need such systems, they are not designed to provide a loyalty-building experience.

2. *I am not a deal; I'm a person.* Once a lead is passed to a Sales Force Automation (SFA) program, the job is to manage these opportunities to close as many as possible. I can see why sales reps need (or at least tolerate) such systems, but it doesn't do anything for me. You see, I'm only concerned about whether my needs are met, not whether I'm a good deal for the rep.

3. *I am not an incident; I'm a person.* When something is broken, getting it fixed quickly is, of course, important. Service/support systems can certainly help. But I don't want to feel like I'm just another number in the system. A little empathy and personal caring goes a long way.

Formal research backs this up. In 2003 Dick Lee, David Mangen, and I did an ROI study on CRM projects and concluded that about two-thirds were "successful." Successful at what? Turns out that most managers expected that CRM would deliver strategic benefits like customer loyalty (the number-one expected benefit) followed by gaining a competitive advantage and increasing sales growth. All important business objectives, to be sure.

Unfortunately in our research we found that CRM's strategic promise was largely unfulfilled. Instead of helping build more loyal customer relationships, CRM mainly delivered tactical benefits, such as improved efficiency, cost reduction, and better decision-making. This is one key reason for the dissatisfaction with CRM performance over the years and why reports of CRM failure were rampant.[7]

More recently, IBM presented one of the most straightforward and realistic CRM definitions:

CRM strategy, enabled by processes and technologies, is architected to manage customer relationships as a means for extracting the greatest value from customers over the lifetime of the relationship.[8]

In the past few years, as customers have empowered themselves with the social web, some CRM proponents have presented Social CRM as a strategic makeover that is all engaging with social customers and collaborating to create mutual value. In a sense Social CRM is yet another valiant attempt to get businesspeople to think strategically about CRM. But, unfortunately, tacking "Social" on the front end of a technology-slanted term didn't change the mind-set.

My 2010 research found sky-high expectations that Social CRM (broadly speaking, the use of social business applications to support customers, partners, and other external relationships) will improve the customer experience and increase loyalty. But most Social CRM use cases are just a social media update to marketing, sales, and service automation. In other words mainly intended to generate leads, manage deals, and handle service incidents.[9]

In the right hands, social technologies *can* help brands engage, deliver value, and build more meaningful relationships. But businesspeople are slow to change, and it's far too easy to apply new tools to old thinking.

Which brings us full circle. *If you treat your social customers like leads, deals, or incidents, Social CRM won't help build customer loyalty, either.*

What Are We Managing?

Customer-centricity is a bit like art. Hard to define, but we all know it when we see it! Unfortunately there's no standard definition. Let's dig a bit deeper into what customer-centricity means and review some history.

One retail executive told me she hated the term "customer-centricity" because it was often used as a meaningless platitude. We've all seen phrases like "The customer is always right" or "The customer is king." Looks great on posters, sounds uplifting in a speech, but it's not enough to create customer and business value.

CEM expert Sampson Lee says customer-centricity means attempting to satisfy every customer need, which "consumes too many resources, reduces customer happiness, and homogenizes brands."[10]

He has a point. If you view customer-centricity as reacting to customer requests without consideration for the brand you want to build and the customers you wish to serve, it is indeed a recipe for failure. Fortunately I've found few business leaders take such an extreme view.

Don Peppers, a founding partner of Peppers & Rogers Group, best known for One to One Marketing, says that customer-centricity should be contrasted with product-centricity. While a product-centric company tries to sell an individual product to as many customers as possible, a "customer-centric competitor focuses on one customer at a time and tries to sell that customer as many products as possible."[11]

> Despite proclamations that CRM is a strategy, the view on the street is that CRM means using tools to extract more value from a customer base.

Professor Peter Fader of The Wharton School of the University of Pennsylvania takes a similar stance in *Customer Centricity: Focus on the Right Customers for Strategic Advantage*. He writes that CRM (which he considers a manifestation of customer-centricity) "represents a firm's front-line efforts to gather data and better understand the unique characteristics and expected value of its focal customers and to use that information to appropriately allocate resources." According to Fader, Apple is not customer-centric because it's a product company. Costco is not customer-centric because it doesn't understand individual customers. Starbucks is not customer-centric because frequent customers of one store can't visit a new store and say, "I'll have the usual, please." In other words, if you're not tracking customers individually, you can't be customer-centric.

I agree with Fader that CRM is *one* manifestation of customer-centricity, but it's incomplete. Although he discusses customer-centricity, it's mostly from an inside-out orientation—what's good for the company. There's little emphasis on what drives customers' perception of value and how to create loyalty. The focus is not on value delivery but rather *value extraction*: capturing and using data on individual customers.

This line of thinking has defined CRM for the past fifteen years. Despite proclamations that CRM is a strategy, the view on the street is that CRM means using tools to extract more value from a customer base. Tactics typically include targeted marketing campaigns, automating sales processes, and cutting service costs. Research firm Gartner more accurately defined this concept as Technology-Enabled Relationship Management (TERM) before CRM caught on as the industry buzzword in the late 1990s.[12]

Let's be clear: Most top-performing companies do CRM really well. But if your CRM project is only about maximizing the return on customers, it can leave those same customers wondering, "What's in it for me?"

Customer Experience Management

In the 2000 to 2005 timeframe, the CRM industry headed in a more tech-centric direction. I felt something was missing. At CRM conferences vendors were mainly demonstrating sales automation. This was fine for the sales manager but missed the larger point—how does this help customer relationships? (Sales professionals had their own set of complaints about the "big brother" nature of sales force automation projects.) CRM really meant Customer *Revenue* Management.

In 2005 I started researching Customer Experience Management (CEM). At first I wondered if it was just another buzzword invented by consultants. After digging into the topic more deeply, and conducting my own study in 2006, I concluded that CEM was fundamentally different from CRM:

> CEM helps the enterprise see the customer with the "right brain"—concerned with perceptions, feelings, and interactions that are harder to quantify but oh so valuable, nonetheless.

Instead of just looking at how valuable the customer is to the enterprise, CEM requires an inspection of the enterprise's value to the customer. Rather than recording transactional information like leads, opportunities, and average handle times, as many CRM systems do, CEM maps the experience from the customer point of view.13

Since that study, there's been an ongoing battle for buzzword domination. Those that go to market under the "CRM" brand (generally technology-focused consultants, analysts, and vendors) tend to say that customer experience is just part of the CRM framework.

In the CEM world, the industry has been driven mainly by consultants who position CRM as just a system you need to support certain technology-enabled experiences (e.g., contact center, websites). CEM is the bigger concept, CEM proponents argue, because it encompasses the entire end-to-end customer experience, including all interactions, touchpoints, and people. In some cases even products!

> Instead of just looking at how valuable the customer is to the enterprise, CEM requires an inspection of the enterprise's value to the customer.

To be sure, both concepts have evolved. In recent years, CRM has become more "social"—which could mean using social media or being collaborative (win-win). Ironically CEM has taken more of a technology slant, which has caused some consternation among consultants, fearing that vendors will turn the concept into a "solution." Indeed, major software vendors have shifted from CRM to CEM marketing messages, along with notable vendors in the contact center, voice of customer, web content management, and social analytics spaces.

So which is the dominant concept? In a 2012 interview, I put that question to Ed Thompson, a Gartner analyst who helped develop the "Eight Building Blocks" of CRM: vision, strategy, valued customer experience, organizational collaboration, processes, information, technology, and metrics.[14]

In recent years he's become Gartner's lead analyst in CEM. Thompson positioned CRM and CEM "like a Venn diagram...adjacent, overlapping, but different."

> Most people would agree that CRM has something to do with sales, marketing, customer service roles in an organization. In other words, the finance guys aren't doing CRM. You could debate that, but it's largely about those three departments.

> But the goals are very long, and we typically collect every six months a list of about forty to fifty what are your goals, your CRM initiative? So, it could be acquisition of customers and cross selling and up selling and learning customer service, the campaign response rate. There's a whole long list of things that people try to achieve.

> Customer experience, I would argue that the goals are narrow, along with the subset of CRM. The goals are advocacy, satisfaction, loyalty.[15]

Analysts at Forrest Research have similar views. CEM analyst Paul Hagen wrote in an April 2011 report: "Typical CRM efforts take an inside-out approach that serves specific business needs but does little to improve or manage customer experience."[16] CRM analyst William Band agreed that CEM was more concerned with how the customer perceives and feels about all interactions with a company but also says (and I agree) that CRM and CEM are not mutually exclusive.

CEM expert Bruce Temkin defines customer-centricity as the "ultimate destination" that is achieved by mastering four competencies:

- **Purposeful leadership:** Leaders operate consistently with a clear, well-articulated set of values

- **Compelling brand values:** Brand attributes drive decisions about how you treat customers

- **Employee engagement:** Employees are fully committed to the goals of your organization

- **Customer connectedness:** Customer feedback and insight is integrated throughout your organization[17]

I certainly agree with Temkin that customer-centricity "cannot be accomplished through an executive decree or a handful of isolated projects." Where I differ is that I see customer-centricity as a *journey* with different stages of development (discussed further in the last chapter on Leadership).

Another distinction is that I believe customer-centricity is fundamentally about *total value delivery*, not just about improving customer interactions, the main focus of Customer Experience Management proponents (see "Create" chapter for more on how customers perceive value).

Managing the Yin and Yang of Customer Relationships

Both CRM and CEM are important concepts. One is not subservient to the other. I think yin-yang is the best way of thinking about these two ideas. On a CustomerThink discussion, business consultant Maz Igbal says yin-yang is about a balanced "middle way," such as:

Balancing the short term with the long term. Balancing hard (data, metrics, analytics, IT) with the soft (people, conversations, human touch, love, compassion). Balance between creating value for customers and value for the stakeholders in the business. Balance between the needs/reward of shareholders and that of the people who create that value through their hard work—employees.[18]

Customer-centricity should be about delivering value for customers that will eventually create value for the company and its stakeholders. For those struggling to position CRM and CEM, I hope this yin-yang concept will help.

Habit 1—Listen

Seek first to understand, then to be understood.
—Stephen Covey

Most would consider Starbucks to be customer-centric. But one time I felt let down by our local Starbucks. Several times a week, my wife and I go for a walk in our neighborhood, and we usually buy a coffee and latte.

Since we tended to stop in the evening, we started noticing that about thirty minutes before the store officially closed, employees brought the tables and chairs from outside and piled them up in the store. Frankly it made the store look like "we're closing" and customers weren't welcome.

After a few experiences like this, I decided to do something about it. Starbucks prominently displays a feedback card saying "Share your thoughts with us" and listing a variety of ways to give feedback. Including, believe it or not, the personal name, phone, and email address of the district manager. I wrote a polite but pointed email to the manager one evening, including this key point: "I feel that if we come into a store ten minutes before closing, we should feel just as welcome as in the middle of the day."

Well, I'm happy to report I got an email response in less than twenty-four hours. He thanked me for the feedback and said he'd review with the store manager. Then they acted. Fast! That evening, tables and chairs were left outside until closing. And what do you know, there were customers actually using them!

From my point of view as a customer, Starbucks is customer-centric because it listened—to *me*.

Measure Twice, Cut Once. What Really Drives Loyalty?

It's all well and good to listen to customers, but listen for what? Unless you know what truly *drives* customer loyalty, surveys may be a waste of time. Especially if customer feedback leads to changes that actually hurt customer loyalty and revenue.

For example, what if my feedback to Starbucks had been to suggest they start selling hamburgers? Should Starbucks have acted on my request in the name of customer-centricity? Of course not.

OK, that's a hypothetical and perhaps far-fetched example. Here's a real one. Consider Walmart's "$1.85 billion mistake," what some experts say the retailing giant lost in an ill-conceived "Project Impact" to reduce inventory. The initiative was a well-intended response to customer feedback criticizing clutter in the stores. The unhappy result, after spending millions of dollars in store refurbishment, was a *decline* in same-store sales.[19]

Walmart's mistake was taking customer feedback at face value without understanding what matters most to its customers. True, some customers complained about clutter. But it was Walmart's broad selection (and low prices) that brought them back to shop, again and again. Moving away from that brand promise, perhaps reacting to a new competitor (Target), was a very expensive mistake.

Over the years in numerous CustomerThink studies, we have found that the customer experience drives loyalty about equally with the function and quality of the core product/service being purchased. Obviously there are differences between industries. You might expect that the customer experience is more critical to Disney than, say, a light bulb manufacturer! Price is also a factor, of course. But except for a few brands like Walmart, it's not a major loyalty driver even though customers will almost always ask for lower prices in surveys.

> Walmart's mistake was taking customer feedback at face value without understanding what matters most to its customers.

Consumers weigh many factors when making a purchase decision. For example, when I bought a new barbeque grill I chose a Weber grill due to its innovative design (product). But I purchased it from Home Depot because it had the best "click and mortar" purchase process (experience). In another case I vented about a frustrating AT&T DSL customer service experience. Although the interactions (experience) with AT&T people were mostly well handled, the core problem is simply that the DSL line (product) was unreliable and no one could figure out why.

Here are a few examples of what really drives loyalty in different industries, based on research from loyalty experts who were kind enough to share some of their work.

Automobiles

I've bought quite a few cars over the years, starting with a used '66 VW Bug when I went to college. Thinking back over all those car purchases, I bought the cars because of the, um, *cars*. Not the dealer experience. Not the service experience.

For some it's all about the car. But for others the dealer experience matters a lot, too. Chris Travell at Maritz Research says that carmakers continue to innovate but find it hard to get an edge with their products. As a result you will find several cars with similar features at any price point. But there are still large differences in the customer experience, so car manufacturers are focusing more attention there. American cars have historically delivered a good experience at the dealer, including greeting customers, sales hand-offs, product knowledge, and delivery. Customers with the highest level of customer satisfaction are five times more likely to repurchase, says Travell.[20]

I agree that customer experience is an important factor, and as cars become more commoditized, it can be a key differentiator. But does that mean the dealer experience is the main *driver* of customer loyalty? David VanAmburg of the ACSI says in terms of relative impact on loyalty, "research shows that it's vehicle quality first, then price, then lastly the dealer experience." A customer experiences a car's quality every time it is driven. Monthly payments of a car loan or lease are also repeating experiences. By contrast, the car purchase experience is a one-time event, and even service experiences are relatively infrequent. Higher frequency is the key reason, says VanAmburg, that vehicle quality is the main loyalty driver for cars and other durable goods.[21]

This makes sense to me as a consumer, because when I'm in the market for a new car, the quality, styling, performance, and reliability are all top of mind and price is the filter for what I'm willing to spend. The dealer experience is more of a tiebreaker. If I can find the car I want at more than one dealer, the best dealer wins. If a dealer sells multiple brands that are somewhat similar (such as domestic dealers selling GM and Ford), then the dealer experience is more critical.

What this means is that carmakers must keep their foot on the gas (pun intended) to build high-quality and stylish cars that incorporate the latest technologies. And then *also* invest in the dealer experience as an opportunity for differentiation.

Retail Banking

Are you delighted when a hotel has clean rooms? With a rental car company if the vehicle runs? With a bank if the ATM works? Not really, because these are basic expectations. But if these table stakes are *not* provided, you'll be dissatisfied and more likely to take your business elsewhere.

That's why Howard Lax of GfK Customer Loyalty advises clients to analyze the negative drivers of dissatisfaction separately from the positive drivers of loyalty. The idea is to minimize the impact of "dissatisfiers" that can drive attrition and focus on loyalty "enhancers" as a way to differentiate.

GfK's banking industry research found that drivers can change from year to year. In 2011 "reward customers for their loyalty" became a new *dis*satisfaction driver. Banking customers now *expect* to be rewarded; it's not a good opportunity to delight customers or drive loyalty. In contrast "helps you be smart about money" is a new positive loyalty driver, which suggests banks should invest more attention here.[22]

Not surprisingly customer experience is a critical issue in most any retail industry. In a retail banking study, Bain found "promoters cited 'service' over six times more frequently than 'rates and fees' or 'branches' as their top reason for recommending." Furthermore, "poor service delivery topped the list of factors named by detractors, with 'rates and fees' not far behind."[23]

Information Technology

Customer intelligence consultancy Walker has studied loyalty drivers in the IT industry for many years. In 2011 43 percent of customers were assessed as "truly loyal"—likely to increase their spending and recommend the IT vendor to others. But Walker's research also found that 26 percent of customers were "trapped"—unhappy with the relationship (attitude) but planning to continue to do business (behavior) anyway.

This is a blind spot for many companies that confuse customer retention with genuine loyalty. Customers that are not emotionally engaged are like time bombs that will eventually explode. As soon as their contract expires or other exit barriers are removed, they will leave! And in recent years even retained and assumed loyal customers can damage a brand by venting their frustrations on social media and other public channels.

2011 IT Loyalty Results

Source: Walker

But what specific factors drive loyalty in the IT industry? According to Walker's 2011 research, "product quality" was at the top of list, with "account management" growing in importance. Walker analysts think this may signal customers' desire to "reap even more from their IT investment during lean economic times." Furthermore, the firm's research found that in 2011 professional servicing/consulting and technical support continued to be an apparent driver but that the purchase process decreased in importance.[24]

At Cisco they review loyalty drivers annually to make sure perceptions are current and make adjustments. Karen Mangia, who heads up Cisco's Listening Services Center of Excellence, says research revealed that "ease of doing business" had become a more important issue. This prompted the company to explore how to get all relevant business units to make changes that will improve customer/partner loyalty.[25]

Loyalty research is not a "do once and use forever" initiative. Your market and customers are constantly changing so regular updates to loyalty drivers are advised.

Wireless Telecom

As a final example, let's look at what drives loyalty in the wireless telecom industry based on research by Bob Hayes of Business over Broadway. His methodology considers three types of loyalty:

- **Retention loyalty:** Degree to which customers will remain as customers or not leave to competitors. This type of loyalty impacts overall customer growth.

- **Advocacy loyalty:** Degree to which customers feel positively toward/will advocate your product/service/brand. This type of loyalty impacts new customer growth.

- **Purchasing loyalty:** Degree to which customers will increase their purchasing behavior. This type of loyalty impacts average revenue per customer.

29

Hayes found that across the entire industry sample, both "product" (wireless coverage and reliability) and "experience" (customer service) had a strong and nearly identical impact on advocacy loyalty, with similar and lower impact on the other two types of loyalty.

However, drivers can vary considerably from one wireless carrier to the next. As Hayes explains: "Improving the service experience is much more valuable for Safaricom than it is for T-Mobile. I suspect the reasons for variability across providers in what drives their customer loyalty could be due to company maturity, the experience delivery process, market pressures, and customer type."

General industry research can give you the big picture, but it may not explain what drives loyalty specifically with *your* customers.

Don't Forget the Basics: Quality and Price

A Forrester Research study on brand engagement found that in brand interactions, more than 50 percent of US online consumers say "they are or may be willing to pay a higher price for a product or service from a brand that is able to impress them with its customer interactions."

What does it mean to "impress" a consumer? The top three reasons to recommend a brand were:

- Good quality of products and services (59 percent),

- Good value of products and services (54 percent), and

- Good discounts, deals, and promotions (51 percent).

What about customer service? Roughly 30 to 40 percent of consumers who said they "frequently" or "sometimes" recommended a brand, product, or service did so because of customer service/support that was "knowledgeable," "fast or convenient," or "friendly."[26]

This report proves once again that driving consumer loyalty is not as simple as providing great service. Providing "the right stuff" at a fair price is still critical.

Creating Raving Fans

Customer loyalty is complex because people and business are also complex. As these examples illustrate, every industry has a different set of dynamics that can change rapidly. Consider how Apple has reshaped expectations in mobile telecom, or how Amazon.com has set new standards for excellence in online retail.

The point of good loyalty research is to understand what *drives* genuine customer loyalty in your target market. Then you can build a strategy to decide where to invest, which will depend on your capabilities and the actions of competitors in your market. Furthermore, you can define customer listening programs to request feedback on what really matters.

While there is no one "best" method for finding loyalty drivers, in my research of top-performing companies, I find that leaders are obsessed with asking and answering these questions:

- What do customers in our target markets really *value*?

- Which issues make our customers unhappy and cause them to *leave*?

- What pleases customers and causes them to *recommend* us to others?

- How can we turn customers into true *advocates* for our business?

Market research and Voice of Customer surveys can help you answer these questions so you'll know what to measure and be prepared to pull the right loyalty levers.

The Ultimate Loyalty Metric for Your Business

Loyalty experts agree that genuine customer loyalty is more than just repeat-buying behavior. A positive attitude is also important because it leads to recommendation and referrals. That's why it's critical to correctly measure customer loyalty so that appropriate actions can be taken.

In 2006 Fred Reichheld's book *The Ultimate Question* proposed a simple method to measure loyalty called the Net Promoter Score. Based on re-sponses on a zero- to ten-point scale, customers are grouped into *promoters* (nine or ten), *passives* (seven or eight), and *detractors* (zero to six). Subtract the percentage of detractors from promoters, and, voilà, you've got a Net Promoter Score (NPS).

With that, Reichheld asserts, you can get rid of those long surveys and expensive loyalty researchers. Just focus on improving your NPS and your company will grow. Prominent brands like AmEx, GE, and Intuit have embraced the method and many others have followed suit.

Simple or Simplistic?

NPS critics contend that Reichheld went too far, dumbing down cus-tomer loyalty into a single, overly simplistic measurement. Jim Barnes of BMAI Strategy reviewed fifteen loyalty models used by major corpora-tions and found three groups of factors: functional, experiential, and emo-tional. "Reducing loyalty to a single number is laughable," he said.

Indeed, other loyalty experts dispute Reichheld's assertions that NPS is the "best" metric. Timothy Keiningham of Ipsos Loyalty found that the ACSI (American Customer Satisfaction Index) and NPS offer similar predictive capability using Reichheld's own data:

> Simply put, we found no support for the assertions attributed to Net Promoter. Our research clearly shows that claims of Net Promoter's superiority in predicting firm growth, or in predicting customers' future loyalty behaviors, are false. Based on the evidence we've compiled, it's hard to imagine a scenario where Net Promoter would be classified as the superior metric.[27]

Larry Freed of ForeSee Results found in an online study that just 1 percent of over twenty thousand people surveyed were likely to communicate a bad experience, whereas the NPS scale estimated that 27 percent of respondents were "detractors." If they aren't talking to other people and/or they aren't saying bad things, they can hardly be considered detractors or "bad profits," says Freed. His conclusion: NPS doesn't cause growth but, rather, is "spuriously" correlated to growth, while the real growth "driver" was customer satisfaction.[28]

> The point of good loyalty research is to understand what *drives* genuine customer loyalty in your target market.

Loyalty researchers also agree that NPS has statistical shortcomings. Why go to the trouble of asking people for a zero-to-ten rating then throw away information by categorizing their responses into three buckets? A simple mean (average) score would be more reliable, meaning it has less statistical error.

Respected academics have found little support for NPS in independent research. In the paper "The Value of Different Customer Satisfaction and Loyalty Metrics in Predicting Business Performance," professors Neil Morgan (Indiana University) and Lop Leotte do Rego (University of Iowa) found that "metrics based on recommendation intentions (net promoters) and behaviors (average number of recommendations) have little or no predictive value." The most effective measurement? Again, average satisfaction scores.

Reality Check

All that said, NPS has rapidly gained popularity and can work for some companies. Intuit, one of the most customer-centric companies around, is a Net Promoter advocate. To understand *why* customers are promoters versus detractors, Intuit uses text analytics to mine write-in comments from TurboTax users. Now you've got the best of both worlds: a very short survey with diagnostic capability.[29]

FileNet, a content management vendor acquired by IBM in 2006, had years of experience with customer loyalty programs. FileNet used to calculate a "loyalty index" but switched to NPS and found it easier for the organization to understand and more effective to drive change. What's more, FileNet has been able to link NPS improvements to revenue growth, according to company officials.

But many companies initially drawn to the simplicity of NPS are changing it to suit their unique business needs. In short, they don't use the "just one question" methodology that Reichheld recommended. In my interviews with NPS adopters, nearly all tell me that they don't rely on NPS exclusively.

Thermo Fisher Scientific spent several years refining its loyalty management approach. Tricia Rakiey, global customer allegiance leader, said the company was initially drawn to the NPS concept but added critical questions for diagnostic abilities: overall customer satisfaction, ease of doing business, likelihood to repurchase, and likelihood to recommend.

And, of course, some companies don't rely on NPS at all. Egg, a European provider of digital banking and financial services, found that asking if the interaction with Egg "made me feel my time was well spent" provided results that helped managers make better decisions on corrective action needed.[30]

Recommendations

Unless you want to bet your business on one magic number, invest in the research required to know what really drives loyalty in your target market. Also remember that any loyalty metric doesn't cause growth; it's just an indicator. Make sure it's one of the key "dials" on your business management dashboard, in balance with other key business measurements.

Here are some recommendations to get the most out of your efforts to measure and improve customer loyalty:

- Keep surveys as short as possible but not too short. Depending on the situation, long surveys can work quite well. But for transactional surveys, limit to a few questions (five to ten).

- Make sure surveys include the *right* questions—those that link to improved business performance and provide adequate diagnostic capability on underlying loyalty drivers.

- If you decide to rely solely on NPS, validate it with common sense and some history. Not so sure? Then hedge your bets by also asking questions about overall satisfaction and likelihood to repurchase.

- Brand your metric and make it your own. Develop an internal marketing campaign to explain what the metric means (no statistical arguments, please) and how it helps the organization succeed.

- Reward managers and employees for improving customer loyalty but don't overdo it. If you make the rewards or penalties too strong, you'll stimulate unwanted "gaming" behavior.

- Plan to evolve and refine your measurements and rewards. You'll need to make adjustments over several years to keep it working just right.

Which brings us back to the key question: Is there one "ultimate question" that will effectively measure customer loyalty for all businesses? No.

The "ultimate answer" is that you must figure out the right metrics for *your* business. What is at stake is nothing less than your customers' loyalty—and your future success.

The Voice of Customer Command Center

Many years ago as a business unit executive at IBM, I was assigned an account that was expected to develop into a $50 million opportunity. We had a crack team assigned and everyone was busy, but I wasn't entirely sure that our relationship was on track. So I set up a meeting with the CEO to ask, "How are we doing?"

Although he said everything was "fine," his body language told me a different story. I dug deeper to get the real scoop and, needless to say, we got busy taking action on the CEO's top issues. Ultimately the relationship prospered beyond our expectations.

Nothing beats a face-to-face meeting to get customer feedback. Some researchers think that words express only 7 percent of human communication. The other 93 percent includes how the words are spoken to convey emotion and body language such as gestures, posture, eye movement, and facial expression.[31] Emoticons aside, it's hard to convey a raised eyebrow or shrug in an email!

Obviously large enterprises with thousands or millions of customers won't find face-to-face meetings a practical means of customer feedback. So customer surveys are commonly used to collect feedback, often with the help of Enterprise Feedback Management (EFM) systems. But surveys are just one of the six dimensions of feedback you can use to understand the health of your customer relationships.

Ground Control to Major Tom

For space launches NASA needs a facility to bring mission feedback into a central location for analysis and decision-making. Likewise chief customer officers need a Voice of Customer (VoC) Command Center to cope with today's multi-channel world. In most cases a VoC Command Center can be a virtual resource. Short-sleeved white shirts and buzz cuts are optional!

In addition to surveys, customers and prospects "speak" *explicitly* to your business via information captured from website forms, unstructured text in comments or emails, and audio recordings of call center interactions. And that's not all. Customer behavioral data from CRM and other transactional systems are examples of *implicit* communication that can signal when a customer is likely to defect—a critical bit of feedback these days when retention is a top priority.

Of course the hot new communications channel is social media, which can also be used as a source of real-time feedback on what customers and market influencers think of your brand. At Gatorade, for example, marketers built a mission control center with six big monitors to display social media data and visualizations from Twitter, blogs, and other public sources.[32] Dell launched a similar social media ground control center to track conversations and internalize the feedback.

This is the right concept, but monitoring social media separately is as limiting as only listening to customers via survey responses. We have enough silos already. The time has come to implement a next-generation VoC Command Center to holistically manage *all* feedback channels.

Voice of Customer Command Center

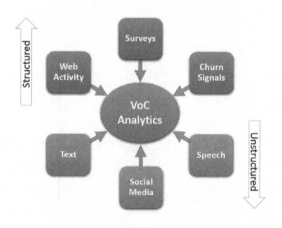

© Copyright 2014 CustomerThink Corp.

Six Feedback Dimensions

Customer feedback comes in many forms. In some cases solicited by the company, such as survey invitations. But over the past few years, unsolicited and often unstructured customer feedback has become more important. As shown in the chart, a VoC Command Center should handle:

- **Structured feedback:** Surveys, web experience data, and churn signals are mostly *data* that can be easily processed with conventional information systems.

- **Unstructured feedback:** In their raw form, text, speech, and social media need help from analytic tools to become actionable information.

Let's review each feedback dimension in a brief tour of a VoC Command Center.

Dimension 1: Surveys

Customer surveys remain a solid foundation for any VoC program. Well-designed surveys sent to known customers can capture key loyalty indicators and dig into specific issues. Specialized EFM systems deliver the survey invitations, collect the data, identify high-priority responses, and alert management to issues needing attention. Some customer service and contact center vendors offer integrated feedback capability.

There's just one catch: Customers won't always fill out your surveys. After a recent trip, I got several survey invitations but didn't complete any of them. One hotel launched a survey from the TV after an in-room checkout process. Nice idea, but after the first question I noticed seventeen more to go. My taxi was waiting, so I abandoned the survey. Other surveys were too complex or showed up so late I couldn't remember what had happened.

Dimension 2: Web Activity

My US consumer study in 2009 found that two-thirds of considered purchases started with a search engine. After searching, the most popular first contact was the company's website (40 percent). Do you know how your web visitors like their online experience? Of course, you could pop up a survey invitation or use specialized widgets to invite customer input. But that may not work in certain situations.

To illustrate, consider how online banking has become a vital part of banking experiences. Consumers like the convenience, and banks want to reduce their cost of operations. A store visit or phone call is far more expensive than a web transaction and wastes customer time.

Some banks record the user's complete web session then analyze recordings to reveal changes in key trends, such as conversion or transaction rates. If problems are identified, managers can dig deeper to find the root cause. Service reps are also better prepared to help when customers call because they can replay the complete online session.[33]

Dimension 3: Churn Signals

Customers are speaking to you implicitly via their behavior, captured in the footprints they leave behind in your systems. One often-overlooked form of feedback can be mined from transaction and historical data already being captured by CRM and other systems.

For example, UK-based telecom firm Orange wanted to proactively reach out to customers at risk for defection because cutting churn by one percentage point could increase profits by 5 percent. Using speech analytics, Orange categorized calls based on customer complaints, requests for account cancellation, technical issues, repeat calls, professionalism issues, long periods of silence, heightened emotion, and service issues. This information was then used to create a predictive analytics model as a kind of "early warning mechanism to accurately and rapidly identify operational and service issues." Using this model, 80 percent of the customers identified as "at risk" had *not* been identified by agents or other systems.[34]

> Customers are speaking to you implicitly via their behavior, captured in the footprints they leave behind in your systems.

Another company that sold prepaid cellular phones had an attrition rate of 12 percent per *month*. As a result, the *company churned its entire customer base* every year. Predictive analytics found a correlation between the sales channel and the defectors. It turned out that consumers who bought their phones at mass marketers hadn't been shown how to replace their phone cards when they expired so they just stopped using the phones. The company worked with its mass-market channel to improve consumer education and make it easier for customers to purchase replacement cards. Result: A 65 percent drop in the attrition rate.

Churn models are popular in financial services, retail, telecom—any industry where consumer retention is a top priority to maximize customer lifetime value. In the telecom industry, predictive churn models can be built based on common reasons for defection, including contract expiration, service quality issues, handset change desired, or competitive offers. In banking, churn models would likely consider changes in account balances and interaction patterns.[35]

Dimension 4: Unstructured Text

Some analysts estimate that unstructured data is 80 percent or more of enterprise information, including documents, emails, web content, etc. Customers contribute their fair share to this information tsunami by completing comment fields in surveys, emailing complaints, or filling out website forms. In the call center, transcribed call recordings and agent notes are other potential sources of unstructured text feedback.

Until the past few years, it was too difficult to analyze a large amount of text feedback. Recent advances in packaged text mining solutions help business managers uncover whether written text has a positive or negative tone (sentiment analysis) and identify specific issues that caused the consumer to vent (categorization). Text mining is not perfect (for example, sarcasm is hard to decipher), but with proper setup may yield 70 to 80 percent accuracy.[36]

Intuit made pioneering use of text mining of comments in survey responses from TurboTax users as part of its NPS-style listening strategy. JetBlue's ice storm fiasco in 2007 compelled it to implement text analytics to analyze forty-five thousand comments per month. In the past few years, the text mining industry has matured, with major tech vendors introducing solutions designed to analyze text, along with many specialized technology providers.

Dimension 5: Speech

Despite the shift to digital channels, the phone remains a preferred interaction method for many consumers. Ironically, so-called *Voice* of Customer programs haven't traditionally included the customer's actual voice—routinely captured in call center recording for many years. Large call centers record calls for quality management purposes, as input to employee coaching/improvement programs.

In recent years speech analytics vendors have emerged to uncover what those calls really mean. Speech analytics is now available as a component solution from multi-function contact center vendors or from specialty providers.

While methods vary between vendors, the core idea is the same: figure out the meaning of spoken words captured in audio recordings. For instance, Blue Cross of Northeastern Pennsylvania has used speech analytics to learn that the root cause of excessive call volumes was system problems and poorly designed processes.[37]

Dimension 6: Social Media

My travels include the usual assortment of good, bad, and ugly experiences. Like many consumers I use social media to give praise for surprisingly good service or to express disapproval.

For instance, after a poor checkout experience at Caesars Palace in Las Vegas, I blogged about my dissatisfaction and included a video of long lines of frustrated customers. The hotel gave no indication that they heard my voice. Worse, on my next hotel stay the checkout process was still broken![38]

That's a shame because complaints in social media are a gift. They hold a goldmine of insights that can help a company upgrade service, innovate, and improve its competitive position. The challenge, of course, is dealing with the massive quantity of social information from blogs, forums, Twitter, Facebook fan pages—any publicly available web resource.

In recent years the IT industry has responded with a wide variety of solutions to capture, monitor, and act on the deluge of social voices. Depending on the application requirements, companies can deploy solutions from social media (brand) monitoring, text analytics, business intelligence, and even CRM vendors.

Getting the VoC Mission under Control

Summing up, there are robust solutions for each of the six feedback dimensions. While each deserves special treatment, the next-generation VoC Command Center must pull them all together with capabilities to:

- *Capture* feedback data across all channels and sources, both explicit and implicit

- *Analyze* feedback to identify breaking trends and customers needing attention

- *Manage* the top-priority issues to a successful resolution

Furthermore, once data is brought together, specialized cross-channel analytics solutions can identify and model the actual path taken on customer interactions. This can explain why customers start interacting with an interactive voice response system (IVR) or website and then abandon to call a (more expensive) live agent. Solving cross-channel problems, according to Sprint's VP of customer experience, Jerry Adriano, can save large B2C companies millions of dollars in unnecessary phone calls while improving customer satisfaction.[39]

Chief customer officers must get a complete picture of the health of their customer relationships. If your organization has been managing feedback independently by channel, it's time to start building your VoC Command Center.

Closing the Loop with Social Customers

Before a 2011 speaking tour, I invested quite a bit of time trying to find hotels that fit my requirements. TripAdvisor reviews were a key input to my booking decisions.

I'm not alone. Each month over fifty million people visit TripAdvisor, according to comScore Media Metrix. And these reviews, flawed as they may be, really do matter. In 2009 a BDRC survey found that nearly half were influenced in their hotel selection by consumer reviews.[40] Two years later another study found that in eight cases out of nine, TripAdvisor Popularity Index was positively correlated with RevPar (Revenue Per Available Room).[41] This research helps quantify the growing power of "social customers" and why companies can't afford to ignore social media.

Best Western Joins the Conversation

Best Western International (BWI) is a major hotel brand with over four thousand hotels worldwide, each independently owned and managed. It's not a franchise, however, according to Michael Morton, Best Western's VP of member services. BWI corporate chiefs can't just dictate what the hoteliers do. Decisions are made more "democratically" by members serving on various committees.

BWI has struggled with negative online reviews. They concluded that it's not enough to have someone in marketing monitor brand buzz at headquarters, which is how most social media monitoring solutions are used. The real issue is *closing the loop* with a consumer who has posted a negative review before it can damage the brand's reputation.

While each hotel may be part of a large brand "family," the day-to-day operation is run by a harried manager who doesn't have time to monitor social media feedback. But waiting for a complaint to be routed from Best Western's headquarters staff was too slow and not "guest friendly," says Morton. To be more responsive to guest issues, BWI members developed a collaborative solution whereby they empowered BWI headquarters to resolve issues immediately if possible. If not, then headquarters staff would connect with the hotel manager to work things out.

"I Care" Is More Than a Slogan

In 2007 Best Western launched the "I Care" customer care training program for its North American hotels. Later it was expanded to help international members.[42] An integrated feedback management solution was implemented to deliver surveys, analyze responses, and distribute feedback to hotel managers.

But this only addressed *solicited*, survey-based feedback. Unsolicited social media feedback—on review sites like TripAdvisor but also Facebook, Twitter, and many more—started as a trickle a few years ago but quickly turned into a torrent. Best Western explored specialized solutions to monitor social media but found solutions too expensive and, more important, not integrated with the feedback management system they had worked so hard to implement. So Best Western co-developed an integrated solution with its EFM vendor that enabled a hotelier to see feedback from both surveys and social media on one dashboard.

Taking Action

The real key, of course, is *acting* on that feedback. Let's say a guest has a bad experience at a Best Western hotel and then posts a scathing review on TripAdvisor. The EFM system harvests and analyzes the social data, associates it with a specific hotel, then sends an email alert to the hotel manager. The manager can then read the review and respond directly to TripAdvisor via an integration.

> The real issue is *closing the loop* with a consumer who has posted a negative review before it can damage the brand's reputation.

In 2008 the Best Western's ACSI score (a measure of overall loyalty) was an anemic seventy versus the industry average of seventy-five. Since then BWI has made good strides improving the guest experience to meet its stated goal to "lead the hotel industry in customer care." In 2010 BWI was ranked the top midscale hotel brand in Brand Keys' Customer Loyalty Engagement Index and earned a "Better Than Most" rating from J.D. Power's North America Hotel Guest Satisfaction Index Study. By 2013 Best Western's ACSI had improved an impressive nine points to seventy-nine, just three points behind industry-leader Marriott.[43]

My family has noticed the improvement. Best Western has come to mean a quality, cost-affordable hotel experience, quite a change in a few short years. Feedback and action made it happen.

Lessons Learned

This story shows how leadership, collaboration, and technology can come together to improve the customer experience and a company's competitive position. Here are the key learning points:

- Best Western's leadership, specifically the CEO David Kong, decided to focus on customer care and then backed up the rhetoric with a major investment in the I Care training programs.

- The BWI headquarters staff and hotel managers collaborated to respond more quickly to guest issues. A command and control management structure was not required to make change happen.

- Likewise BWI and its VoC systems vendor worked together to "co-innovate" a new solution. A good example of the vendor listening to its customer, using this opportunity to expand its product portfolio.

- Finally, this story shows how integrating multiple feedback channels can improve insight and simplify the lives of frontline managers. That's why companies need a Voice of Customer Command Center.

FOOD FOR THOUGHT

- What are the key drivers of *your* customers' loyalty?
- Are you using both solicited and unsolicited feedback?
- Do you listen to your customers' digital behavior?
- Are employees measured and rewarded for customer loyalty improvements?
- Do you systematically close the loop between feedback and action?

Habit 2—Think

*The conventional view serves to protect us from
the painful job of thinking.*
—John Kenneth Galbraith

Of the five habits of customer-centric leaders, I suppose "think" is my favorite. Maybe it's because of my analytic bent from an early age, leading to a degree in mathematics and an MBA that emphasized statistical analysis and operations research. I've always been intrigued with using methodologies and tools to solve problems.

Or perhaps I was influenced by IBM, where I was employed for over fifteen years. IBM founder Thomas J. Watson Sr. actually created the THINK slogan as a sales manager at NCR in 1911. Frustrated at the lack of good ideas at a meeting, he proclaimed: "The trouble with every one of us is that we don't think enough. Knowledge is the result of thought, and thought is the keynote of success in this business or any business." After joining IBM, he used THINK to foster a culture of using technology to help business leaders make better decisions.[44]

And, of course, CustomerThink Corp. is the name of my firm and www.customerthink.com is where you'll find the online community that has been a key part of my life for more than a decade. The name actually came from community input, when we held a contest to find the best name to convey being focused on customers.

Whatever the reason, I believe that making smart, fact-based decisions is absolutely essential to customer-centric leadership. I'm sure many of you reading this will say to yourselves, "We're already doing that."

Sorry, but you're probably not. As you'll learn, many decisions are made out of habit, not conscious thought. And others are influenced by biases we all have.

Read on and you'll also understand why I don't advocate analytics or technology as the be-all-end-all to effective decision-making. Human judgment will never go out of style. Not every insight can be put into a spreadsheet, analytic model, or computer system. In fact, the explosion of so-called "big data" and analysis tools will stretch human decision-making skills, not make it easier.

Oh, the Thinks That We Think

We humans often think we think better than we actually do. Why is that?

First of all, how can we make rational decisions about customers when customers themselves don't make decisions rationally? In his provocative 2008 book *Predictably Irrational*, behavioral economist Dan Ariely argues that people don't always make decisions by rational choice, carefully weighing the benefits of a potential action against the costs. David Berreby sums up nicely in a *NY Times* book review:

> Yes, you have a rational self, but it's not your only one, nor is it often in charge. A more accurate picture is that there are a bunch of different versions of you, who come to the fore under different conditions. We aren't cool calculators of self-interest who

sometimes go crazy; we're crazies who are, under special circumstances, sometimes rational.[45]

Just to pick one example from a book full of myth busters, consider how "decoys" influence our decision-making. We are constantly looking at things in relation to others and tend to avoid comparing things that cannot be easily compared. Ariely illustrates this phenomenon with a story about honeymooners choosing between three travel packages: Rome with a free breakfast (A); Rome without the free breakfast (B); or Paris with a free breakfast (C). Instead of rationally comparing the free breakfast options for both Rome and Paris, people will tend to pick Rome with the free breakfast because it's clearly superior to a similar alternative. Option B is known as a decoy because it serves only to make option A more attractive.

The implication for business leaders is that consumers are harder to convince to do something dramatically different even when it is a much better alternative. The safer route, in the short term at least, is to present choices similar to those already available in the market. That's probably one reason why we see "New Improved!" labels on products with minor updates and few breakthrough products.

There's another factor at work: *habits*. A 2007 Duke study concluded that we are on automatic pilot for nearly half of the choices we make each day. According to the study, "features of a person's context (e.g., people, places, and preceding actions) can be powerful, automatic triggers of habit performance and that habits are executed with minimal recourse to conscious monitoring."[46]

> We aren't cool calculators of self-interest who sometimes go crazy; we're crazies who are, under special circumstances, sometimes rational

Also take note of the groundbreaking work of Nobel Memorial Prize winner Daniel Kahneman, who summarized decades of research on human thinking and behavior in a 2011 book, *Thinking, Fast and Slow*. He found that we humans use two systems for thinking:

- **System 1**: Fast, automatic, frequent, emotional, stereotypic, subconscious

- **System 2**: Slow, effortful, infrequent, logical, calculating, conscious

Even in conscious "System 2" thinking, people struggle to think statistically. For example, we are prone to overestimate benefits and underestimate costs. We are easily swayed by a small sample of readily available data that supports something we want to do and ignore other factors that should be considered.

This "optimistic bias" encourages us to take on risky projects. Perhaps that's why a good rule of thumb in IT project planning is to take the most conservative (highest) estimate of time and costs and then double it! Projects almost never get done on time because we don't allow for *unknown unknowns*. If you don't believe me, take a look at your last home remodeling project. I'll bet it cost at least twice as much as you budgeted because of problems that surfaced after you started.

Torturing Data to Tell Lies

I know what you're thinking. "Here comes a pitch about why computers and analytics hold the answer to human shortcomings." Sorry to disappoint, but statistics can be just as misleading. As economist Ronald Coase famously said, "If you torture the data long enough, it will confess."

A classic case of statistics abuse was published by the San Francisco Chronicle, when a journalist wrote about the United States lagging behind other countries in average Internet speeds. With the US "limping behind Latvia and the Czech Republic" in ninth place, he concludes this is "troubling news" because studies link faster Internet connections to the economy. Doubling Internet speeds would increase GDP by .3 percent, or $126 billion, for the US economy.[47]

Was the columnist taking creative license with the report findings? Sadly, no. I reviewed the full report, sponsored by Ericsson, and found these conclusions in the section "The Socioeconomic Impact of Data Speeds."

- Doubling the broadband speed for an economy increases GDP by 0.3 percent.

- Eighty new jobs are created for every thousand new broadband connections.

- For every 10 percent increase in broadband penetration the GDP growth is around 1 percent.[48]

Should you take the report at face value? You might want to consider that Ericsson is a provider of technology to telecom operators, so it has a vested interest to look for conclusions in the data to "sell" the impact of faster Internet speeds.

The report says it used regression analysis, a statistical technique that attempts to relate one or more independent variables (broadband speed, in this case) with dependent variables (economic impact). But correlation doesn't imply causation. While it may seem reasonable that advanced economies use technology more aggressively, it doesn't follow that technology usage literally *causes* economic growth. In my view, broadband speed is probably just one of many different growth enablers including roads, bridges, power, and schools.

Actually, it's quite possible that cause and effect work in the *opposite* direction. As economies grow, businesses decide to invest in faster Internet speed. The correlation would look exactly the same.

Confusing correlation with causation is one of the more common mistakes in using analytical techniques. Yet correlation is frequently used to promote the idea that some new technology or trend will lead to business success. Rarely is the research done in a way to show true cause and effect.

For example, excellence in Customer Experience (CX) is often promoted as driving business performance. Jon Picoult of Watermark Consulting compared the total stock market returns of top ten ("leaders") and bottom ten ("laggards") publicly traded companies in Forrester Research's annual Customer Experience Index ranking. He concluded that for 2007 to 2012, CX leaders "outperformed the broader market, generating a total return that was three times higher on average than the S&P 500 Index."[49]

The problem with this study, like many others, is that it's just a simple correlation. While I agree that a better CX is probably one factor in business success, it doesn't follow that CX is the only reason or the main "driver." When I've examined practices of companies that lead their industries, I find they are more adept at a number of disciplines, including leveraging technology, process management, using analytics, and being more social or collaborative. In fact, most every popular management discipline can show a correlation to business performance.

> Confusing correlation with causation is one of the more common mistakes in using analytical techniques.

Unlike the ACSI research mentioned earlier, Picoult's research isn't predictive—it doesn't show that CX improvement is followed by improved business performance. And correlations don't prove that CX is the *only* factor involved in driving success. In fact, ACSI research and other loyalty studies show that product quality and price/deals continue to have a strong influence on customer buying and retention.

Other common mistakes that confound people attempting to draw conclusions from data:

- **Over extrapolating results to a larger population.** Let's say you collect online survey responses in the United States. Should results be extrapolated worldwide, including people who don't use the Internet? Probably not, although I've seen this done frequently.

- **Drawing conclusions from insignificant differences.** In a political poll, if the difference between candidates is within the margin of error, there is no "winner," statistically speaking. But I rarely see margins of error or statistical confidence levels reported in business research.

- **Failure to use a control group.** Suppose a marketer finds a particular sales incentive is correlated with higher revenue. To verify that offer is what's driving sales and not something else, the incentive should be given to an experimental group while an otherwise identical control group is left alone.

Data Scientists to the Rescue?

Getting valid insights from data and analytics requires specialized training and a lot of experience. The expanding world of "big data," an IT industry term meaning the increasing volume, velocity, and variety of digital information, has elevated the role of the so-called data scientist. IBM sees this role as an evolution of a business analyst. Training should include technical skills such as computer science, math, modeling, and statistics. But a data scientist should also have the business skills needed to identify valuable problems to be solved and influence business and IT leaders to make the right decisions.

That's a tall order. McKinsey estimates the United States faces a shortage of 140,000 to 190,000 analysts. Furthermore, a much larger 1.5 million professionals lack the skills needed to "understand and make decisions based on the analysis of big data."[50] To close the gap, I believe that business leaders need to push their own professional development so they can ask better questions and avoid common analytic pitfalls. Analytics vendors must also address the skills gap by making solutions more usable for business managers.

Using Analytics to Improve the Consumer Experience

Despite our best efforts to collect and analyze data, good business decisions will always include elements of judgment, intuition, or just plain

Types of Business Analytics

Descriptive — What happened?

Predictive — What will happen?

Prescriptive — What should happen?

luck. Many day-to-day decisions are made with little or no thought because the option selected just seems "right." Gut-feel decisions might be examples of what Malcolm Gladwell called "thin-slicing" in his provocative 2005 bestseller *Blink*.

However, the best decision can sometimes be counterintuitive. For example, the financial services firm Assurant Solutions wanted to improve its "save" rate on customers calling in to cancel their protection insurance. The industry's conventional wisdom was to focus on reducing call center wait time to boost customer satisfaction, which resulted in 15 to 16 percent retention rates. But data analysis found a better solution: matching customer service reps with customers based on rapport and affinity tripled the retention rate.[51]

Business leaders are also turning to analytics to uncover insights in so-called big data. However, big data is like a vein of gold buried under your feet. Unless you can mine it effectively to improve business performance, all that data could be a worthless distraction.

Analytics is a terms applied broadly, perhaps too broadly. The most common form is descriptive analytics used to slice and dice data to understand what happened in the past. There are an enormous number of tools that can be used, from Excel to sophisticated server-based software designed for major enterprises.

But increasingly attention is turning to forward-looking analytics, using specialized algorithms and software. The Assurant Solutions example just mentioned is an example of predictive analytics. Prescriptive analytics take it a step further and attempt to actually *influence* the future. For example, analytics can be used to help a call center agent decide the best offer to present to a customer to increase the odds of making a sale, or to suggest actions to deal with a service issue.

Macy's Journey from "Mad Men" to "Math Men"

Macy's is a great example of a major retailer competing for the loyalty of "omnichannel" shoppers—those using multiple channels, such as retail stores, websites, mobile devices, and even social media. Five years ago, the company began a customer-centric shift, led by Julie Bernard, group VP of customer centricity.

Speaking at a 2012 conference, Bernard said her goal was to "put the customer at the center of all decisions." Sounds good, but old habits die hard in a 150-year-old brand where data was organized around products. The retailer used POS data to analyze product sales but couldn't figure out what individual consumers were doing. One simple example: Did a spike in sales of a new pair of jeans mean the product was a hit or that one person bought all twelve pairs in a store?

Initially Bernard's data-based attempts at busting myths about consumer preferences were largely ignored. The turnaround came when CEO Terry Lundren got more personally involved as a self-appointed chief customer officer. You can also see the crucial role of data analytics in Macy's definition of customer-centricity:

1. CEO sponsorship for the ongoing use of customer data

2. Data analyzed to guide strategic customer focus

3. Data organized into customer languages to unify the organization

4. Data leveraged to inform customer insight activations

By also looking at data from loyalty programs, credit cards, and other sources, Macy's was able create a more complete understanding of the products, pricing, and experiences that move "loyals"—those consumers already buying regularly. In the future, Bernard thinks analytics can also help the retailer make smarter decisions about the $40 billion spent annually on merchandise, a much larger expenditure than marketing.

Improving Online User Experience

Imagine you are responsible for expedia.com, a complex website that serves millions of travel shoppers each month. How would you improve the user experience and increase the percentage of shoppers that book online?

Let's say you want to present shoppers with hotel options in a major metropolitan area like New York. According to then Expedia VP Joe Megibow, most users won't do a complex search of hundreds of hotels, so it's critical that Expedia put the "best" options at the top of the list. If your instincts told you to present the cheapest or more popular hotels first, Expedia would frustrate a lot of shoppers and lose bookings.

Analytics determined the factors most likely to meet customer demand, such as real-time availability, inventory by class, rate deals, reviews, and purchase frequency. Then, using technology from an analytics software vendor, Expedia built a predictive analytics model based on the handful of factors that really mattered, out of about two dozen possibilities. The model was operationalized using Expedia's own proprietary technology. Result: When consumers search NY hotels, they're more likely to find the hotels that they really want, and Expedia will get the sale. A great example of technology enabling a win-win.

Optimizing Marketing Spend

One of my favorite retailers, Nordstrom is an old company that is embracing new technologies. At a 2012 analytics conference, James Steck of Nordstrom's Advanced Analytics group discussed how the retailer used analytics to understand product and brand relationships. The idea is simple: Figure out how to promote the right products and brands to the right customers, maximizing revenue in the process.

Perhaps a simple idea, but not an easy problem to solve when you've got a busy website along with 225 stores doing around $10 billion in sales annually. Certainly not a decision that could be made effectively by "gut feel."

Nordstrom analyzed two thousand consumers over a one-year period, covering 164 brands. They found 50 percent of shoppers bought brand A. How then can the retailer find those more likely to buy brand B? Turns out that analytics could identify that a group of customers spending more than $187 had a greater likelihood to buy brand B. Armed with that insight, marketers could make more effective merchandising and promotion decisions to increase sales.

Analytics can also be used to optimize email marketing. Gilt Group's Tamara Gruzbarg says the retailer is using analytics to influence merchandising and promotion strategies. The heritage of the retailer is upscale "urban fashionistas," but as the company has grown and expanded, it has become more challenging to make smart decisions. Email remains a critical promotion channel even as users adopt mobile devices. One predictive model that paid off helped Gilt tune the email frequency based on engagement and age indicators to maximize revenue while minimizing unsubscribe rates.

Improving Product and Service Quality

Jim Bampos, as VP of customer quality at EMC, led the firm's efforts to leverage big data to improve both product experience and customer experience. The EMC "total customer experience" includes every step of the customer/partner journey (buy-deploy-use-service), as measured by surveys and customer quality metrics. EMC uses analytics to predict product failures so they can be fixed before impacting the product experience. Reported issues can be very complex, so getting to the right expert is critical.

In customer service, analytics also helped EMC make two key improvements. First, they learned that a "chase the sun" approach wasn't effective because handing off complex problems to another support center in another part of the world meant poor continuity with customers. Opening a 24/7 global support center in Utah solved that problem. Second, EMC found that it was misguided to focus on time to answer a call. Analytics revealed that the total time to *solve a problem* had a bigger impact on customer loyalty.

Toward Better Decisions

What makes big data most interesting to me is the new types of information such as website clickstream data, social media posts, video surveillance feeds, and even sensor data from consumer products. These new forms of data definitely pump up the volume, requiring new data storage techniques such as Hadoop, open source software for managing very large data sets across clusters of computers. New analytics tools have also been introduced to analyze most any kind of data you can collect.

However, what's "big" about big data is open to interpretation. According to analytics expert Karl Rexer:

For some of our clients, we certainly have analyzed over a million US tax returns or tens of millions of bank transactions or grocery store transactions. Now, to us those seem like big datasets, and that seems in a way to be big data and big data analysis. But if you were Google, Facebook, or Amazon, or looking at web traffic, or

61

if you're in a scientific field looking at some astronomy data or some genome research, you might have data that's much larger and different. Sometimes it's wide, in terms of lots of columns, or very deep in terms of the number of rows. And so other people's data might be far larger than the datasets that we've been using.[52]

Big or small, more data doesn't necessarily mean better decisions. The key is picking right decisions, says James Taylor of Decision Management Solutions. The biggest mistake is to start with the data or the technology, rather than the decision. "Big data projects should focus on how to improve how we run the company," advises Taylor.

A recurring theme from industry experts is the importance of knowing what's possible. While so-called data scientists are emerging in high-impact positions designed to mine big data effectively, I believe the real leverage is in *data strategists*. These are business leaders like Bernard and Megibow who focus on key decisions that improve the customer experience and/or increase profitable revenue.

> The biggest mistake is to start with the data or the technology, rather than the decision.

Everyone seems to believe that "thar's gold in them-thar hills." I wonder, though, if the excitement around big data will follow the same path as the Great Gold Rush of the 1850s. Miners flocked to California in search of gold, but most came up empty. The companies that made money were the suppliers of picks, shovels, and what came to be known as Levi's jeans.

To sum up, big data *is* a big opportunity, but the challenge is focusing analytics on the big decisions customers will care about. Otherwise, you'll end up with fool's gold, not the real thing.

Mining Unstructured Text to Find Golden Nuggets

Text mining, like its geological counterpart, is sifting through vast amounts of debris to find the gold. As noted by Ronen Feldman and James Sanger, authors of *The Text-Mining Handbook*, what we call "unstructured data" isn't completely unstructured: text follows some basic tenets of natural language. Text mining means analyzing text to 1) determine what the original author was trying to say or 2) learn something completely new.

Like data mining, the idea is simple, but what's "under the hood" in text-mining applications can be very complex. One common technique is called "categorization," which has been used since the late 1960s in areas such as medicine and news services. A simple example would be deciding whether customer emails represented "happy," "unhappy," or "neutral" customers, based on the types of words used in those emails.

In recent years, text-mining algorithms have been more widely adopted by businesses, thanks to Moore's Law, which drives continued computer performance improvements. But equally importantly, the setup and usage of text-mining systems have become much easier with the adoption of packaged and on-demand solutions.

Executives at companies that are using text mining to analyze their unstructured customer feedback are enthusiastic about the benefits. For them, not only did text mining help them meet the challenge they knew they had, but they also found numerous other uses and benefits.

Listening Drives Improvement at JetBlue

At JetBlue, text mining was introduced as a result of the infamous New York ice storm of 2007. After being overwhelmed with fifteen thousand emails in just two days, a text-mining vendor helped the airline learn that customers were upset about the delays and cancellations and disappointed that JetBlue didn't have a backup plan. On a more positive note, some customers wrote to compliment airport staff and in-flight crews on their handling of a difficult situation.

Since that crisis, JetBlue has worked to more systematically mine customer sentiment, as well as providing "tangible data around how to augment JetBlue services," according to Bryan Jeppsen, the airline's customer feedback analyst. By tying feedback data to a specific aircraft or even a seat number, they can find and fix problems that have a direct impact on the customer experience.

More generally, contact center executives are looking for more effective tools to address customer experience and operational performance issues. When creating customer feedback, "we took a pretty decent stab at anticipating what our customers might want to tell us," said Meredith Sime, associate director of customer experience with AT&T's U-verse, a new platform for services provided over Internet Protocol. "But we did not initially invest enough resources in mining the wealth of information from an unstructured format."

Those instincts were borne out once they started analyzing the data. "We learned a tremendous amount of information that helped us drive improvement plans, and it taught us to ask better questions."

If your customers are suffering from survey fatigue, shorten surveys and provide more opportunities to provide comments via your website, chat sessions, emails, etc. Then use text analytics to listen to customers on their terms, so you can act on emerging issues long before you could field a conventional survey.

Capitalizing on Fresh Insight

If you've eaten at a restaurant or shopped at a store lately, you may have seen an invitation on your receipt to call a toll-free number and respond to a survey about your recent experience. Surveys are now commonplace tools for companies to solicit customer feedback. Most surveys allow customers to add their comments. Other sources of text feedback include call center agent logs, transcripts from recorded phone calls, mobile (SMS) text messages, email messages, chat sessions, and posts on discussion forums or blogs.

If you give customers a chance, they'll communicate with you in many ways. Garden Fresh Restaurant Corp., a chain of 104 buffet-style restaurants, wanted to take better advantage of this valuable feedback. In addition to inviting customers on restaurant receipts to take surveys, Garden Fresh posts a toll-free phone number in its restaurants, inviting customer feedback. Customers listen to the voice prompts and rate the restaurant experience. Guests are also given the opportunity to record a sixty-second message, which is also transcribed.

With so many vocal customers, the company was overwhelmed by the volume of customer feedback. It was cost-prohibitive to manually process about ten thousand pieces of unstructured feedback a month from the different channels. Company leaders worried that if they were soliciting feedback and not responding to important information in that feedback, they were wasting people's time or, worse, angering customers.

In 2005 Garden Fresh began working with a text-mining vendor to find meaning in all that feedback. It took the company about three weeks to set up shop, enabling new monthly "praise" and "complaint" reports, both showing trends and drilling down to individual customer comments. One "aha!" moment early on was in responding to customers' demands for more soup varieties, including vegetarian soups. The company expanded the number of soup varieties offered, and complaints about variety lessened.

Maximizing Your Success

Start by truly committing to act on the feedback you receive, whether it's structured or unstructured. Even if the answer is "no," customers appreciate knowing their feedback was received and considered.

Also make sure your project has senior-level sponsorship. A customer-centric vision will help, because it may be difficult to "prove" in an ROI spreadsheet exactly how your company will increase revenue or cut costs by investing in text mining. After all, part of the value of analytics is finding *unknown unknowns*.

Picking the right solution is critical for two reasons. First, in text mining algorithms do matter, so you'll need to invest some time to understand if what's going on "under the hood" is generating valid insights for your specific use case. But second and equally important, any tool you select must be easy to use or adoption will be limited to analytics professionals.

Text analytics is not just about automating a process to gain efficiency. Progressive business leaders see text analytics for customer feedback as a necessary part of a customer-centric enterprise. What golden nuggets of information are hidden within the customer feedback your organization collects?

Use Speech Analytics to Reduce Frustrating Calls

The sluggish global economy has driven business leaders to tighten budgets in all areas, including contact centers. Does the customer experience need to suffer? Not necessarily—if cuts are made with a scalpel instead of a machete.

One "scalpel" that can help is analyzing the audio from recorded customer calls. It's a great way to listen to the "voice of the customer" by listening to the actual *voice* of the customer. No survey required! Speech analytics can reveal opportunities to fix the root cause of problems, which can save money and improve the customer experience at the same time. That's a win-win for your customers and the bottom line.

If you've ever called a customer service department for help, you've probably heard a message: "Your call may be recorded for quality assurance." Perhaps you've wondered, what happens to those call recordings?

Blue Cross of Northeastern Pennsylvania wanted to learn why its customers were calling. Sure, agents can note in their records that customers were calling about a benefit, claim, or other issue, but according to customer service director Bob McDonald, those notes didn't give him "actionable items to work on." So in 2007 he used a speech analytics solution to "mine" audio recordings to find the root cause of calls.

For example, Blue Cross used speech analytics to understand the reasons for extremely high call volumes. McDonald was able to validate that, in one case, it was the result of something anticipated—a recent system change. The data gave him "ammunition that the problem really needed fixing." In another case, McDonald discovered, much to his surprise, that customers were circumventing processes to get faster service. Armed with this insight, McDonald changed the call flow and improved agent training.

Speech recognition and analysis technology has been around for quite some time, with applications in government, security, and call centers. Contact center analyst Donna Fluss of DMG Consulting figures that 2004 was the year it "burst into the commercial world," with a grand total of twenty-five implementations. By 2007 that figure had grown to more than twelve hundred implementations. In 2013 and beyond, Fluss predicts double-digit growth rates for the speech analytics market, helped along by increasing interest outside of the contact center.

It's not just about saving money. Fluss contends that speech analytics can also improve the customer experience—a key factor in customer loyalty and retention.

Contact center analyst Keith Dawson of Frost & Sullivan shares this optimistic outlook. Contact centers have traditionally been concerned with improving agent performance, including staying "on message" and offering the correct up-sell or cross-sell offers. Speech analytics can help in these areas, of course, but Dawson notes that most call centers and marketing departments have not "parsed the customer side" of calls. Now technology makes it possible to understand how customers are responding to the agent, including their emotional state.

Smart Practices

Industry experts agree that a sluggish economy could accelerate the growth and adoption of speech analytics in contact centers. The main driver is the need for operational efficiency, but increasingly business leaders recognize that the customer experience is critical, too. Even when consumers are spending less, service quality will factor into their buying decisions.

To have the best chance for success and getting a fast payback, consider these four tips:

- Given that budgets will almost certainly continue to be squeezed, plan to use the insight gained to make wise choices about where to cut costs, where to fix problems, and which customer segments need different treatments.

- Because this is still a relatively new market, make vendor decisions carefully. There are the usual trade-offs between full suite and specialty vendors. Likewise, the technology "under the hood" does matter, so invest the time to understand which methodology fits your requirements best.

- Speech analytics experts give much the same advice that applies to CRM projects: Take small steps toward your grand vision. Pick an application to learn from, prove out the ROI, and then expand.

- Most importantly, Fluss counsels you to ensure your speech analytics project is staffed appropriately. Done right, you can get a return in three to nine months.

Budgets cuts may be a painful reality as businesses try to optimize resources. The good news: You don't have to share that pain with your customers. Use insights gained from speech analytics to improve the customer experience while operating your call center more efficiently. Then your customers will stick around to do more business with you instead of leaving for your competition.

Harmonize the Cross-Channel Service Experience

Remember the "good old days" when if you wanted to interact with a customer you had a meeting, made a phone call from your office, or sent a letter?

Well, those days are long gone. Starting with email in the 1980s, then fax, mobile phones, chat, SMS, and now social media—we keep adding new electronic channels. Why? To provide more convenient service and, let's be honest, to cut costs. E-channels are much cheaper than agents on the phone or other human-assisted interactions.

All too often interactions aren't coordinated across channels, leading to customers repeating themselves as they move between channels. To further complicate matters, now we have social channels (e.g., Twitter for customer service), which are not under the company's direct control.

If you're a large enterprise selling to thousands or millions of consumers, I'm willing to bet that it's a bigger problem than you realize. My 2009 study of "considered purchases" with US consumers found that 70 percent of large enterprises admitted they don't remember customer information from one touchpoint to the next. And 78 percent of consumers reported that information had to be repeated during complex (multi-touch) service experiences.

Interesting statistics, but so what? Well, consumers exposed to companies suffering from this "touchpoint amnesia" were *50 percent less likely to recommend* that company and had *24 to 35 percent lower purchase rates*. This should not come as a surprise, since other consumer studies have found a top customer frustration is having to speak with several agents and starting over each time.

Cross-channel analytics

One of the more advanced uses of analytics is optimizing the cross-channel customer journey. Interaction data is usually managed in silos, and you can't easily get a complete picture of what's happening as a customer navigates multiple channels.

Customer service is a prime opportunity for cross-channel analytics. Companies want their customers to use automated channels to save money. But this can be "penny wise and pound foolish" if the cross-channel experience is not well designed.

In 2007 the mobile telecom company Sprint achieved unwanted notoriety by firing its unprofitable customers for making excessive support calls. Unfortunately, leaders failed to account for the media backlash. Worse, firing "bad" customers didn't address the core issues of *why* those customers were calling and therefore unprofitable.

Well, Sprint engineered a remarkable turnaround by systematically uncovering and fixing customer service problems. The process took a couple of years and required top management to finally get serious about improving the customer experience. Lance Williams, Sprint's director of customer management, explained that in 2008 Sprint had the worst interactive voice response (IVR) customer satisfaction in the industry. They used cross-channel analytics to understand why customers were abandoning the IVR to call the agents—a frustrating experience for customers and a very expensive issue for Sprint. After improving customer usability, by Q4 2009 Sprint's IVR customer satisfaction score (CSAT) was leading the industry. That helped the contact center to "contain" (complete interactions in the IVR) "tens of millions more calls" in 2009 as compared to 2008. Translation: Huge cost savings.

> All too often interactions aren't coordinated across channels, leading to customers repeating themselves as they move between channels.

Analytics also helped Sprint learn that "early life" customers who called significantly more often than average had much lower CSAT. So they created a specialized "early device treatment" program that improved first call resolution rates and CSAT—a remarkable achievement considering that devices (smartphones) were getting more complex during this period.[53]

Sprint's improvement has been impressive. In 2008 Sprint's ACSI score (a measure of overall satisfaction and loyalty) was a dismal fifty-six versus an industry average of sixty-eight. By 2013 Sprint's score had improved to seventy-one, a point below the industry average and competitive with other major mobile operators.[54]

The use of cross-channel analytics is becoming more accepted now, but justification can be challenging when managers fight over budgets. At a large technology firm, one frustrated manager told me it took about *three years* for management to get fully on board and finally commit funding. Once they did, analytics showed the true cost of bad cross-channel experiences in agent call-time savings. Similar to Sprint, poorly designed IVR systems forced customers to call an agent for help. This degraded the customer's experience and wasted agent resources.

All Together Now

Odds are that your company is overdue for a cross-channel experience checkup. It's not enough to offer multiple channels and optimize each independently. They should work together in harmony. Like an orchestra with an expert conductor, it's the total experience that matters, not how good an individual instrument sounds.

Before you throw technology at cross-channel experience problems, consider the leadership and organization you have in place. Ideally you should have a customer advocate who owns the end-to-end customer experience and reports to the CEO. Titles like chief customer officer or chief experience officer are becoming more popular, but they will only work if the position is empowered correctly (see the last chapter on customer-centric leadership).

It's also critical to track cross-channel success metrics and link to your compensation and reward system. Otherwise, you'll continue to optimize individual channels owned by departmental silos.

Are you conducting your multi-channel experience with all channels working together in harmony? If not, it's time to figure out just what those sour notes are costing you. This could be just the ticket to create the differentiated customer experience that will save money and increase customer loyalty.

FOOD FOR THOUGHT

- Are you using solid statistical techniques or torturing data to tell you what you want to hear?
- Do your business leaders have the skills needed to interpret analytics and make decisions?
- Are you taking advantage of unstructured information and new sources of big data?
- Are metrics designed to be both forward (predictive) and backward looking?
- Are you applying analytics to both value creation and extraction?

Habit 3—Empower

Want to go above and beyond for a customer? Make a suggestion?
Try something new? We want you to take the initiative, and we'll
support your efforts to deliver exceptional service.
—"Our Culture" at Nordstrom

After a distinguished career at Google, starting as employee number twenty, Marissa Mayer was appointed CEO of Yahoo in July 2012. The challenge was clear—turnaround a struggling web property that had seen years of malaise, executive turmoil, and declining revenue.

In February 2013 Mayer returned from maternity leave and decided to terminate work-at-home privileges. The move sparked outrage and heated debate. Would less flexibility cause top-performing employees to flee and hurt the firm's chances to hire new talent? Or was it a shrewd move that will help the company rally together to collaborate more effectively as "one Yahoo!"—according to the leaked internal memo?[55]

Mayer's decision was controversial because technology has become a popular way to collaborate. Enterprise social networks, web conferencing, and knowledge-sharing applications are now ubiquitous in companies big and small. If these technologies are so great and flexibility is what employees want, then why not just let *everyone* work at home?

74

The simple truth is that technology is still a poor substitute for human interaction. An employee of a company that Google bought told me that work-at-home arrangements were terminated shortly after the acquisition. The acquired company had more flexible working arrangements but was struggling nonetheless. Google management believes that people need to be together for maximum productivity. Although the change brought some grumbles, it seems the majority of employees are happy with the acquisition and are adapting to the "Google way" of doing business.

Has Google's performance suffered? Hardly. Google's business results have been very impressive indeed, a sharp contrast to Yahoo's woes in recent years. What about morale? Google shines here, too. Based on Glassdoor reviews, employees are "very satisfied" overall (4.1 on a scale of 1 to 5) and CEO Larry Page earns a 95 percent approval rating.[56]

Should we conclude, then, that being *less* flexible with employees is the key to boost business performance? Of course not. However, it's also a fallacy that giving employees everything they want automatically translates into improved business performance. (Incidentally, that doesn't work with customers, either.)

The Employee Engagement "Leap of Faith"

Work flexibility is part of the larger issue of "employee engagement," the subject of enormous academic and business research. While there is no one agreed-upon definition, employee engagement is usually thought of as a measure of an employee's job satisfaction and commitment to the organization and its goals.

In the business world, Gallup is a research firm noted for attempting to measure employee engagement with just twelve questions.[57] All relate to how the employee is treated as an *individual*. In my view, Gallup's survey does a good job of quantifying employee WIIFM ("What's In It For Me?"). That's important, but is it really the key to business performance?

Over the years (decades, really) Gallup has pumped out an astounding amount of research, including a meta-analysis that concluded "the relationship between engagement and performance at the business/work unit level is substantial and highly generalizable across organizations." Read that report and you'll be impressed with how well employee engagement *correlates* with business performance.

I emphasized "correlates" because Gallup does not directly state that employee engagement *causes* or *drives* business performance. On the contrary, you'll find this statement on page fifteen: "This paper does not directly address issues of causality, which are best addressed with meta-analytic longitudinal data, consideration of multiple variables, and path analysis."[58]

The selling of employee engagement to the business world is essentially a leap of faith. The process goes like this: 1) measure employee engagement; 2) segment companies (or business units) into degrees of engagement; then 3) compare business outcomes by segments. And what do you know, you can clearly see that companies with more engaged employees also have better business outcomes—like increased revenue and profit, lower employee turnover, better customer service, and so on. Who wouldn't want more of this?

The temptation, of course, is to draw a causation arrow from employee engagement to performance. The correlation is impressive, and it makes intuitive sense. Improve employee engagement and you'll improve business performance. End of story.

What If Business Performance Drives Employee Engagement?

Except for one small problem. Assuming correlation means causation is one of the most common mistakes in analytics (see "Think" chapter for details). While Gallup didn't claim this causation directly, I've seen countless references to Gallup research using the correlation to sell training, collaboration tools, and other technologies. The pitch: "Our solution will improve employee engagement and your business will prosper."

The problem is that a correlation between A and B can result from: A causing B; B causing A; or C causing both A and B. Advanced statistical techniques can help figure whether the chicken or the egg comes first.

Academic research does generally support the argument that employee engagement is a factor in business performance. But you should also take note of a groundbreaking 2003 study by Schneider, Hanges, and Smith—researchers who conducted a longitudinal study with thirty-five organizations over eight years. The surprising finding: *A stronger "causal directionality flows from financial and market performance to overall job satisfaction."*[59]

More recently Gallup studied ten large organizations and concluded: "Results of this study provide support for the proposition that employee perceptions of work cause future organizational outcomes such as employee retention, customer loyalty, and financial performance."

> Employee engagement and business performance have a reciprocal relationship.

However, a careful reading of the study also reveals that "the directional arrow from financial performance to overall [job] satisfaction (.12) is just as strong as the path from satisfaction to financial performance (.11), which suggests a stronger reciprocal relationship from financial performance to the general attitude of satisfaction than we observed with the working-conditions composite (.12 vs. .05)." A more nuanced conclusion can be found in the authors' discussion of the findings:

> The finding of a reciprocal relationship between satisfaction and financial performance is consistent with findings reported by Schneider et al. (2003), possibly indicating that business units with more satisfied employees engage in discretionary activities that may benefit the organization but also that financial success may reinforce satisfaction by leading to better pay, benefits, and job security.[60]

Like many topics in science and business, you can find a study to support your point of view. Mine is that employee engagement is a necessary but not sufficient condition for customer loyalty, which in turn is a factor in business success. Loyal customers also contribute to a more positive employee experience. Employee engagement and business performance have a reciprocal relationship.

Incidentally, while it's too early to render a verdict on Mayer's leadership at Yahoo, after a year on the job, morale increased significantly and so did the stock price. It would seem employees welcome strong leadership that turns the company around; telecommuting flexibility is not such an important factor as some proclaimed initially.

The Danger of "Employees First" Thinking

There may be situations where putting employees ahead of customers makes sense, at least for a time. In this camp is Vineet Nayar, CEO of IT outsourcer HCL Technologies and author of *Employees First, Customers Second*. Nayar explains in a 2012 interview:

I am saying is by employees first you can actually deliver your promise of customers first. If you do not put the employee first— if the business of management and managers is not to put employee first—there is no way you can get the customer first.[61]

While this has a whiff of circular logic, dig deeper and you'll find that Nayar is saying that employees create value for customers, so managers must focus on employees first. In the case of HCL needing to boost morale and trust as part of a transformation, this makes good sense.

Still, I think it's dangerous to take "employees first" literally and extrapolate to all businesses. Consider the fate of "dot bombs" in the late 1990s. Internet visionaries built businesses on the promise of monetizing eyeballs. Until the venture capital money ran out, employees enjoyed parties and working in offices equipped with Aeron chairs, games, and free food.

More recently, Groupon is another cautionary tale. Founder/CEO Andrew Mason was fired for a plummeting stock price and poor business performance just fifteen months after the second largest IPO in US history. Judging by office photos and YouTube videos, employees enjoyed working at Groupon. In Mason's resignation message, he imparted this "wisdom" on employees: "Have the courage to start with the customer." He also wrote that his biggest regrets were "the moments that I let a lack of data override my intuition on what's best for our customers."[62]

Customers or Employees First? Yes!

Let me be clear: Employee engagement *is* important. Employees who are highly committed to their jobs, like their bosses, and feel appreciated will work harder and be more productive. There's no real debate about that.

That said, this critical question remains: *Productive at what?* If employee efforts are not aligned with creating customer value that also helps the organization succeed, it's just wasted energy. And customers, not employees, have the final say as to whether a company is delivering something of value.

Michael Lowenstein, an expert in customer and employee loyalty, argues that companies should move beyond engagement to create "employee ambassadorship," which he finds is "more closely correlated with business results and value-building." Three elements are:

- **Commitment to company:** Commitment to, and being positive about, the company (through personal satisfaction, fulfillment, and an expression of pride), and to being a contributing, loyal, and fully aligned member of the culture

- **Commitment to value proposition:** Commitment to, and alignment with, the mission and goals of the company as expressed through perceived excellence (benefits and solutions) provided by products and/or services

- **Commitment to customers:** Commitment to understanding customer needs and to performing in a manner that provides customers with optimal experiences and relationships as well as delivering the highest level of product and/or service value[63]

Instead of a linear relationship of employee engagement driving business results, or vice versa, I suggest viewing customer and employee engagement as another example of yin-yang in business. Stop debating which one comes first or is more important. Realize that employees and the customers *both* have to be engaged, at the same time, to move your business forward for sustainable success.

Improve Your AIM to Empower Service Reps

On a trip to Orlando two years ago, I arrived quite late to a Hilton hotel and visited the restaurant a few minutes before closing. The server took my order and disappeared—for just a few minutes too long.

I was starting to wonder if my order had been forgotten when the server came back, apologized for the delay, and offered me a free drink. I still remember that experience because it wasn't expected. The delay really wasn't a big deal, and I had no intention of complaining.

It surprised and delighted me that my server was empathetic enough to realize that Hilton's service was not quite up to par, without a complaint. Crucially, he didn't have to ask permission to give me that drink.

That's a simple but powerful example of an empowered employee. My server obviously had some latitude to make a decision on the spot to create a memorable experience. The fact that I've told this story many times in keynote speeches, and now write about it here, speaks volumes for the real impact of that simple gesture.

Empowerment is one of those fuzzy words that can mean many different things. In my view, you need three elements to put the concept to work in customer service: authority, insights, and motivation (AIM).

Authority to Make Decisions on Their Own

If employees can only do exactly what they're told, they're not empowered; they might as well be robots. And make no mistake about it, empowerment really matters to your customers.

A customer-centric research study by Dick Lee and David Mangen found employee empowerment an important factor in "customer focus" behaviors, which were "the most influential in driving purchase selection, and by a wide margin." But the study also found that customer focus includes product quality, and concludes:

> Customers are saying that product strength alone cannot cover up for customer indifference—and conversely, that customer-friendly behaviors alone can't cover up for weak product.[64]

The truth is that I wouldn't go back to Hilton if they screwed up service routinely, even if employees were empowered to placate me with a free drink or another accommodation. That's why it's critical to establish a foundation of product/service quality, and meet it consistently, while also striving to delight customers (see "Delight" chapter).

Even so, "stuff" happens that can't be anticipated, which is where employees that have authority to act can be a tremendous asset. At Southwest Airlines, for instance, leaders believe that employees should use their own good judgment in handling passenger situations. And for the most part, they do. It's one reason that Southwest has been leading the airline industry in customer loyalty for the past eighteen years.

Empowerment means having the authority to make decisions with consequences.

Of course, sometimes employees won't make good decisions. Southwest's management took a lot of heat for poorly handled situations with an overweight Hollywood director and the skimpy attire of a young woman (read more about these situations later in this chapter). Despite blowback on social media, Southwest didn't create a dress code for passengers or write more rules for employees to follow.

Empowerment means having the authority to make decisions with consequences. At Ritz-Carlton, employees have latitude to spend up to $2,000 *per incident* to create an outstanding experience, not just to fix a problem. Notable examples of empowered employees, according to Simon Cooper, president of the Ritz-Carlton Hotel Company, include:

- Hiring a carpenter to build a shoe tree for a guest,

- Flying from Puerto Rico to New York, *twice*, trying to get a stain out of a dress, and

- Building a wooden walkway to the beach for a disabled guest in Dubai.[65]

- Take a tip from Ritz-Carlton and don't reserve these acts of "lagniappe"—a creole word for doing a little something extra—for service recovery. Why not give agents the authority to do favors for valuable customers when they *aren't* complaining?

Insights to Get the Job Done Quickly, on One Call

When I had problems with my DSL, I contacted my provider for help, starting with the self-service website. Finding it too confusing, I decided to post a plea for help on Twitter.

Well, the good news is that my tweet got a quick response and helped me connect with an agent. More good news: The agent clearly had put me into a priority status. Although it left me wondering how my incident would have been handled if I had used normal support channels.

That call took a long time. I don't know exactly what was going on, but I could hear keys clicking in the background interspersed with "we're working on your problem" verbal updates.

My guess is that my hard-working agent was experiencing some version of "Alt-Tab Hell." That's my term for what an Aberdeen Agent Desktop Optimization study found: Agents use an average of five different screens to access the systems needed to serve customers. Aberdeen analysts estimate that 26 percent of agent time is spent navigating systems.

Fortunately, there are solutions that can help agents:

- Virtual contact centers can provide a more usable interface for agents to manage multiple interaction channels, including social media.

- Knowledge management systems can help the agent find an answer quickly, searching multiple information sources while the customer is on the phone.

- For complex problems, an agent can tap the company's social network to find the right expertise and ask a question.[66]

Of course, not all problems can be solved with one contact. That leads me to another customer annoyance—the company forgetting information the customer has previously provided. A 2010 Clickfox study found that the top customer frustration, cited by 41 percent of respondents, was "having to speak with multiple agents and starting over every time."

As mentioned previously, CustomerThink's consumer research found that consumers who had to interact with companies suffering from this "touchpoint amnesia" were 50 percent less likely to recommend that company. To make matters worse, it also wastes agent time when they can't access customer information already provided on a self-service interaction. The solution, once again, requires taking an integrated view of interactions across channels and making this information easily available to service agents when the customer calls.

Of course, the ultimate solution is no service. Figure out why customers are calling and fix the root cause! But until that happy day arrives, make sure agents don't waste time getting the insights they need to help customers on one call.

Motivation to Delight Customers

To paraphrase Einstein, insanity is expecting employees to do one thing while rewarding them for doing something else. A classic example: Executive proclamations to delight customers, while continuing to measure and reward agents who get customers off the phone as quickly as possible. If you've ever been on the receiving end of one of those calls, you know it's anything but delightful.

Still, there's some debate about whether delight is the right strategy. A study by the Customer Contact Council concluded that it's better to focus on reducing customer effort. I disagree because, while low-effort customer service is certainly important to decrease *dis*satisfaction, it's generally not sufficient to build an emotional bond. (See "Delight" chapter for more on this study.)

To put it more bluntly, *not screwing up is hardly a memorable experience*—unless poor service is the norm in your industry. And placating customers with over-the-top service recovery measures is not the only or even the best way to delight customers.

If delight is part of your company's strategy, then your rewards system is absolutely essential to reinforce the right behaviors. The theory is straightforward: People tend to select behaviors that lead to a more desirable outcome. Incentives matter. In practice, it's tricky to figure out what to measure to avoid unwanted "gaming" behavior—like being pressured by a car sales rep to give a ten on a satisfaction survey.

Although companies have talked about customer satisfaction and loyalty for as long as I can remember, measurements and rewards systems have lagged behind the rhetoric.

- An ICMI study in 2006 raised a concern that "only one in five centers surveyed base agent incentives and recognition on the critical metric of first-contact resolution (FCR)." Quality measures more commonly used were quality monitoring scores (83 percent), customer feedback (60.5 percent), and coworker feedback (33.8 percent).[67]

- A 2007 CustomerThink study of loyalty management practices found that in 42 percent of companies, customer loyalty did not "affect employee rewards of any kind." A year later, another survey revealed that just 14 percent of companies "fully" used "performance measures and rewards to encourage employees to treat customers well."

- In 2008 an ICMI study found that 51.2 percent of respondents reported that their center measures FCR for live agent phone calls.[68]

Contact centers have been slowly making the shift from productivity measures like Average Handle Time (AHT). By 2011 an ICMI poll reported about two out of three contact centers tracking FCR—the percentage of customers getting a problem solved on the first call/contact.[69]

Bruce Belfiore, CEO of BenchmarkPortal, says using FCR can have a positive impact on both cost (productivity) and quality (customer satisfaction). Belfiore argues that customer feedback, via a post-call survey, is the best way to calculate FCR. The customer's perception matters most!

Internal measures can also be used. However, assumptions can dramatically change FCR, as call center expert Bill Price writes in a 2013 CustomerThink article:

> Over the years it has proven hard to measure FCR, with efforts to estimate FCR (e.g., "if the customer doesn't call back in seven days, we will declare the earlier contact to be resolved") shown to be imprecise. Some customers/issues need more than seven days to sort out, and other customers might contact the company for other reasons within seven days, and many dissatisfied customers might not place another contact at all.[70]

Once you've developed an operational metric linked to customer loyalty, the key is creating employee rewards and recognition programs that encourage improvement based on that metric. At AmEx, for example, agents are motivated to deliver a great customer experience through rewards and recognition tied to RTF—would the customer they served "Recommend To a Friend." Tammy Weinbaum, senior VP and general manager for the American Express service centers in Arizona and Utah, said they "found that this was really the best metric to hold people accountable for the work that they're doing."[71]

Zappos, the quintessential example of a company striving for delight in call center experiences, uses Net Promoter Score (NPS), but that's not all. In February 2010, according to an insightful post by customer service expert Greg Levin, Zappos ditched a traditional quality-monitoring program and replaced it with Full Circle Feedback (FCF), which was developed collaboratively with call center staff. FCF has five components including self-evaluations, observations from team leads, "calibration checks" to ensure some consistency, sharing and learning from "above and beyond" calls, and NPS feedback from customer surveys.[72]

Culture, the Glue for Customer-centric Behavior

One last point—don't overlook culture. Metrics and rewards are important, but they can be taken to extremes, making people feel like Pavlov's dog.

Many years ago, I remember interviewing an Amica Insurance employee and asking how management rewarded them for providing great customer service. The answer: Nothing. The company's culture expected great service, so delighting customers made employees feel good about their jobs, which was reward enough. Must be working because Amica continues to rack up awards for customer and employee satisfaction.

So that's it. Three practical ways to empower service agents. Give them the authority, insights, and motivation needed to delight your customers. Good luck improving your AIM.

Is Social Software the Cure for Business as Usual?

News flash: Your company is slowly going out of business. Just like the parable of the frog sitting in a pot of slowly warming water. The frog doesn't jump out until it's too late, and it cooks to death.

Think you're smarter than the average "frog"? Then consider an Innosight study of the S&P 500: The average tenure of a firm decreased from sixty-one years in 1958 to just eighteen years in 2012. At the current churn rate, 75 percent of the S&P 500 will be replaced by 2027. Will your company make it?[73]

My point is that surviving for the long term requires innovation and risk-taking. If you're not willing to try something new until it can be "proven" with an ROI spreadsheet, it's probably too late to get a competitive advantage. At best, you'll just keep pace with your fellow frogs, er, competitors.

Innovation, Collaboration, and the Problem with "Social"

One way companies can innovate is to improve the quality of the workforce to work faster, smarter, and—this is the important part—*deliver more value to customers.*

Don Tapscott, in his 2011 white paper "Social Software, What's Next?", astutely observed that "The business world is evolving to a flatter ecosystem to support complex integration resulting in a demand for innovation. Innovation is supported by a culture of collaboration."

To me, collaboration simply means *people working together to accomplish something.* Unfortunately, "collaboration" is too often used as a synonym for using tools. Collaboration tools used to be called "groupware." But in the past few years, the Web 2.0 movement has resulted in a proliferation of so-called "Enterprise 2.0" solutions, a term coined by Andrew McAfee in 2006 and now generally accepted to mean using social software within companies. For customer-related social applications, the term "Social CRM" is used more commonly.

Some use the term "Social Business" to include both internal (Enterprise 2.0) and external (Social CRM) use of social software for business. In either case, the point is to enable better employee teamwork and/ or customer engagement to drive improved business performance. It's not about singing "Kumbaya" around the campfire.

For business leaders who feel a little queasy about creating a "social enterprise," I suggest using "collaborative" instead. People don't come to work to share a la Facebook, just for the fun of it. But modern-day collaboration does involve more social sharing and communications in the *context of getting work done.*

Searching for Social ROI

Since 2007 McKinsey has been researching the adoption of twelve different Web 2.0 technologies. In the 2013 update, the top five technologies used were online video-conferencing (60 percent), social networking (53 percent), blogs (43 percent), collaborative document editing (43 percent), and video sharing (41 percent). Considering what McKinsey found as key benefits, you might think that Web 2.0 tools are a safe bet to deliver ROI:

- For employee usage, the top three measurable benefits cited by respondents were increasing speed to access knowledge, reducing communications cost, and increasing speed to access internal experts.

- For customer usage, increasing marketing effectiveness, increasing customer satisfaction, and reducing marketing costs topped the list of benefits.[74]

That should do it, right? Nothing more to see here, move along and implement your social software and let the benefits flow!

Sorry, but no. Over the past few years, there's been a lot of debate pro and con. In 2009 the curmudgeonly Dennis Howlett wrote that businesspeople "don't give a damn about the 'emergent nature' of enterprise."[75] I agree: Businesspeople care about business results—along with getting promotions and bonuses, of course!

Independent research studies have raised more questions than they have answered. For example:

- CustomerThink's 2010 Social Business study found most enterprises kicking the tires on both Social CRM and Enterprise 2.0, without a strong business case. Generally speaking, expectations of ROI were higher for external (Social CRM) usage. My concerns about unrealistic expectations led me to predict that 80 percent of Social CRM projects would fail to meet expectations.[76]

- Chess Media Group's 2011 State of Enterprise 2.0 Collaboration study found only 20 percent of respondents said they achieved (or nearly achieved) their performance indicators, while 48 percent didn't know—probably because they didn't set and monitor key performance indicators. On a more positive note, 73 percent of respondents said "solving a business problem or achieving an objective" was as good as showing a financial ROI.[77]

- Altimeter Group's 2012 study "Making the Business Case for Enterprise Social Networks" found "an undercurrent of concern about the value creation and sustainable adoption of ESNs."[78]

I hate to say it, but this smacks of the early days of CRM when it got a reputation as a failure. How do you know if you've succeeded or failed without established goals?

Furthermore, the "goals" commonly mentioned for internal social projects were, ahem, a bit mushy. Improved sharing and collaboration has at best an indirect connection to more fundamental business imperatives like increasing sales, cutting costs, or improving competitive differentiation. Maybe part of the ROI problem is that benefits are not more directly linked to creating customer value?

"What Is the ROI?" Is the Wrong Question

After reviewing all the above and much more, I've come to the conclusion that "What is the ROI?" is the wrong question. Fundamentally, improving collaboration is about working differently, which I believe all companies will need to do if they want to survive for the long term. ROI, on the other hand, is a warm and comforting friend of business as usual. Because you can't calculate an ROI on the unknown, can you?

Let's see if Morpheus, from the 1999 science fiction film *The Matrix*, can help me get this point across. He explains to Neo that people are living in a programmed world:

> The Matrix is a system, Neo. That system is our enemy. But when you're inside, you look around, what do you see? Businessmen, teachers, lawyers, carpenters. The very minds of the people we are trying to save. But until we do, these people are still a part of that system and that makes them our enemy. You have to understand, most of these people are not ready to be unplugged.

People don't want to be unplugged from business as usual. It looks normal and safe, but it's just an illusion. Whether you choose to participate or not, the real world outside your business continues to innovate and will eventually entice your customers to leave.

Choose Your Focus: Employees or Customers

After the CRM disappointments of the past fifteen years, it should go without saying that throwing technology at a problem alone won't work. But I'll say it anyway, because the same is true of Social Business technology.

Yet it's also true that, just like with CRM, technology is the enabler. So it's fair to ask: Exactly how will social software (properly focused and implemented) drive value for the organization?

One strategy is to empower employees to improve productivity and engagement. An Enterprise Social Network (ESN) fits this approach. Early adopters extoll the value of an ESN to accelerate employee on-boarding, speed up decision-making, and help people find experts. However, based on all the research and commentary I've read, most companies are *not* doing a formal ROI study before implementing an ESN. Instead, they are investing toward a strategic goal of a more engaged, nimble, and productive workforce.

> Social Business solutions should connect the dots between internal collaboration and customer-facing activities.

A second strategy is to strengthen the customer value chain. A February 2012 Harris Interactive study found that nearly 80 percent of respondents said they use social media sites. Of those, about two-thirds agreed that they'd be able to provide better support to customers/end-users with more collaborative and easy-to-use tools at the workplace.[79]

In other words, tools that help employees *focus on the customer relationship*. Based on CustomerThink research and many other studies, increasing customer-related value—such as revenue, experience, loyalty, etc.—is a well-traveled path to ROI.

These two strategies are not mutually exclusive, of course. Some companies may wish to focus on employee empowerment and invest in a horizontal platform, either enterprise-wide or for specific groups or departments. Others may choose to add a social element to customer service and other CRM applications.

Longer term, it should be "and" and not "versus." Social Business solutions should connect the dots between internal collaboration and customer-facing activities. I believe this integrated approach will separate the top-performing companies from those that just socialize departmental silos.

Blue Pill or Red?

McKinsey's 2012 research found 67 percent of companies with plans to increase Web 2.0 investments over the next three years. Social networks are already in use by over half of companies, along with an array of other tools.

Still undecided about whether to invest in social software? Here is more advice from Morpheus:

> This is your last chance. After this, there is no turning back. You take the blue pill—the story ends, you wake up in your bed and believe whatever you want to believe. You take the red pill—you stay in Wonderland and I show you how deep the rabbit-hole goes.

The safe choice is the "blue pill"—business as usual. Just keep doing what you're doing; don't take any risks until you can get a guarantee that social software will deliver an ROI.

I think the "red pill" looks a lot more interesting. To be sure, there are risks in social software, and ROI is uncertain. But Social Business applications could open up new ways of working, enabling your organization to be more nimble and customer-focused. And who knows, you might even see the woman in the red dress!

Work Backward from the Customer

In the mid-1980s, during my time at IBM, I remember an "empowerment" initiative that swept through the company. We attended training programs and learned that to be empowered meant we had to take more responsibility and be accountable for the results. Over the next couple of years, the strategy unfolded as IBM pushed more authority to lower levels of the organization. Eventually I headed up a "business unit" with P&L responsibility and had more authority to make decisions on discretionary spending.

Looking back, it's not clear to me that these changes had any real impact on our business results. Still, I felt good that IBM gave me a bit more authority. That's an example of what academic researchers call "psychological empowerment"—giving employees a sense of control in how they do their jobs. This can lead to higher levels of job satisfaction, which can boost productivity and increase retention.

Yet despite more empowered employees, IBM performance suffered for many years during that period. The turnaround came when Lou Gerstner took charge in 1993. That year IBM posted a $8 *billion* loss, on top of nearly the same deluge of red ink from the previous two years.

Was the problem not enough empowerment? Hardly. In *Who Says Elephants Can't Dance?* Gerstner writes that he found IBM culture "inbred and ingrown," preoccupied with itself rather than customers.

To make a long and complicated story short, Gerstner changed the IBM culture to be more lean, nimble, and accountable. And, yes, more focused on customers. In 1994 the company earned $3 billion and financial results continued to improve after that.

Gerstner reflected in his last chairperson's letter in 2001:

> Through it all, our guiding light came down to two words: customer focus. It has proved both galvanizing and clarifying, serving as the criterion for reexamining a whole lot of dogma and for resolving many of our seemingly intractable internal debates.

Empowering employees in a business model that isn't competitive won't make the business competitive. You still have to deliver products and services that customers want, do it better and faster than competitors, and manage costs. Empowerment is not a panacea.

What Is Customer-centric Empowerment?

In a business context, empowerment means giving employees more influence and control over their jobs. IBM is not the only company that jumped on the empowerment bandwagon. An academic literature review in 2008 concluded that "more than 70 percent of organizations have adopted some kind of empowerment initiative for at least part of their workforce." The goal of the best organizations is to get employees to take initiative to "serve the collective interests of the company." Academics argue that "social-structural" empowerment is about employees participating though *increased access to opportunity, information, support, and resources.*

Empowerment Practices

- **Participative decision-making:** Employees and/or teams may have input into and influence over decisions ranging from high-level strategic decisions to routine day-to-day decisions about how to do their own jobs.
- **Skill/knowledge-based pay:** Employees share in the gains of the organization and are compensated for increases in their own skills and knowledge.
- **Open flow of information:** Includes flow of information upward and downward in the organization, so that employees have "line of sight" about how their behavior affects firm performance.
- **Flat organizational structures:** Empowering organizations tend to be decentralized where the span of control (more subordinates per manager) is wide.
- **Training:** Educative efforts enable employees to build knowledge, skills, and abilities—not only to do their own jobs better but also to learn about skills and the economics of the larger organization.

Adapted from "Taking Stock: A Review of More Than Twenty Years of Research on Empowerment at Work," by Gretchen Spreitzer (2008).

I see customer-centric empowerment as *giving employees more authority and support to create value for customers.* This is critical because customers like to interact with empowered employees. Said another way: To build customer loyalty, reduce the frequency that an employee has to get approval from the boss to get stuff done!

One obvious application is service recovery. If a customer calls to complain, an empowered employee can take the initiative to offer an accommodation. Ritz-Carlton takes it a step further, empowering employees to spend up to $2,000 to delight a guest—not just to fix problems.

When you call Zappos for advice on an order, you won't get rushed off the call because agents are empowered to spend as much of their time as needed to create a great experience. In one extreme example, the on-line retailer set a new record with a call that lasted over ten hours. The "service" was the agent talking to a customer about living in Las Vegas! A spokesperson wrote later that the call exemplified its core value of "wow through service."

Empowerment is not limited to call centers or service interactions. In the often painful car-buying experience, one sales ploy is "checking with the boss" as part of the haggling process. Much like customers prefer a "one and done" customer service experience, Maritz Research found that car buyers want to deal with as few people as possible: 64.0 percent of customers are completely satisfied when one person with pricing authority negotiates the deal, compared with 20.7 percent when two or more are involved.

Where Does Empowerment Fit?

Empowerment is not abdication. It needs to fit the business strategy and be relevant to the employee's job. In "The Empowerment of Service Workers" (article in *Managing Innovation and Change*, Third Edition), David Bowen and Edward Lawler argue that empowerment fits better when one or more of the following contingencies are met:

- Basic business strategy is differentiated, customized, and personalized

- Tie to customer is a relationship over long time period

- Business environment is unpredictable with many surprises

- People are "Theory Y" managers, employees with high growth needs, high social needs, and strong interpersonal skills

Empowerment is *not* a good fit when a company is working in a "production line" approach. For example, when you go to a quick-serve restaurant, you don't want the employee to be empowered to change how the food is prepared. Consistency is part of the value proposition, whether you're eating a hamburger at McDonald's or sipping a latte at the more experiential Starbucks.

If you shop at an Apple store, you'll probably find the staff personable and engaging, without the hard sell. They don't appear to be robotically following a script, but nevertheless they are intensively trained on what they can and can't do. According to a *Wall Street Journal* article, a training manual instills the "APPLE" approach into every employee: "**A**pproach customers with a personalized warm welcome," "**P**robe politely to understand all the customer's needs," "**P**resent a solution for the customer to take home today," "**L**isten for and resolve any issues or concerns," and "**E**nd with a fond farewell and an invitation to return."

How Technology Can Support Empowerment

It should be clear that empowerment is not about technology, at least not directly. Yet technology is one way to improve access to opportunity, information, support, and resources. Here are a few examples of how technology can support empowerment.

Let's start with listening, one key habit of customer-centric firms. Customer experience expert Lynn Hunsaker of Clearaction found that presenting Voice of Customer survey results to all employees was one of six best practices in high-performing B2B organizations. At Applied

Materials, for example, they created and shared reports throughout the company so that "every sales office and functional area across the company could see their own impact on customer experience." Increasingly, Enterprise Feedback Management (EFM) systems are used to collect, analyze, and distribute customer feedback to stimulate action by the responsible department.

Of course, customer feedback comes in many forms, not just surveys. Customers also share their opinions in social channels, such as blogs, review sites, Facebook, and Twitter—content that can be "mined" using social analytics solutions. Best Western integrated TripAdvisor reviews with traditional survey feedback, so that if a guest has a bad experience and posts a review on TripAdvisor, the "social EFM" system sends an alert to the hotel manager for immediate action.

Empowerment is not just something bestowed by managers. In *Empowered*, authors Josh Bernoff and Ted Schadler recount how employees can *empower themselves* with consumer-grade mobile, video, cloud, and social technologies. One out of three employees use some form of do-it-yourself technology—often not sanctioned by the IT department—including online productivity tools, document management, and microblogging. Organizations that already have a collaborative culture seem best suited to benefit from an Enterprise Social Network (ESN), which advocates say can accelerate employee on-boarding, speed up decision-making, and help people find experts.

In call centers, real-time speech analytics is an innovative way to empower agents to add more value during customer interactions. During a live phone call, technology can analyze the spoken interaction and generate customized actions for the agent to prevent churn, up-sell, etc. This is a huge improvement from rigid scripts that leave customers feeling like they are talking to a machine.

Lean, Not Mean. Southwest's Key to Profitable Growth

One of the biggest misconceptions about customer experience is that it's about delivering a "premium" experience. You know, like Apple, Ritz-Carlton, and Zappos.

It's true some companies win by "wowing" their customers. But a great customer experience can also be a differentiator in low-cost business models. Consider Southwest Airlines, one of my favorite examples of a customer-friendly business that is also low cost.

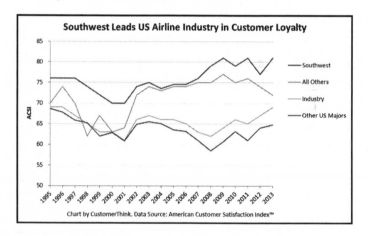

Some have called Southwest a "cattle car airline" because it doesn't offer preassigned seats, unlike virtually every major airline. Hardly a premium experience. How, then, has Southwest enjoyed *four decades* of profitable growth?

Furthermore, as you can see in the chart, Southwest has been leading the airline industry in loyalty ratings (according to the ACSI) for the past eighteen years. From 1995 to 2013, Southwest's gap versus other major US carriers expanded from six to *sixteen* points. That's huge.

How does Southwest continue to earn customer loyalty and consistently make money? I believe it boils down to three things: staying true to its brand, empowering employees, and fair pricing.

Staying True to Brand Promise

When I think of Southwest, I think affordable, dependable air travel, with service provided by friendly people. That's what the brand means to me, because I've experienced it firsthand dozens of times over the years.

It didn't happen by accident. Southwest was founded by Rollin King and Herb Kelleher with a simple idea: "If you get your passengers to their destinations when they want to get there, on time, at the lowest possible fares, and make darn sure they have a good time doing it, people will fly your airline." Company leaders have never wavered from that promise. If customers suggest something that runs counter to their brand promise, the answer is "no." Nicely, of course.

A good example of this is open seating. I'll admit it's not my favorite part of the Southwest experience. Until some refinements a few years back, it seemed like I'd always end up with a center seat in the back of the plane.

But Southwest considers potential service improvements through the lens of its business strategy. Turns out that open seating means faster turnaround time at the gate. Southwest turns airlines in twenty-five minutes versus forty minutes for other airlines, and passenger boarding is one key reason why. Faster turns means they get higher utilization of their fleet, which means lower costs, which supports the low-cost brand promise.

CEO Gary Kelly explained in a 2006 blog post: "Open seating has allowed us to build a highly efficient operation by keeping the time our aircraft are sitting at our gate to a minimum. Aircraft on the ground don't make money!"[80] Fortunately, Southwest did refine their boarding system to support early check-in and assign numbers in A/B/C queues. I'd still prefer an assigned seat, but like many Southwest customers, I'm willing to compromise on that in return for a good deal.

Key point: Being customer-centric doesn't mean abdicating to every customer request. Especially if giving in means undermining the very reason they are customers!

Management to Employees: "We've Got Your Back"

Like many customer-centric brands, Southwest has a distinctive culture. You can trace it back to the colorful founder, Herb Kelleher, a former lawyer who created the business model on the back of a napkin.

Many companies have tried to figure how Southwest managed to create such a loyal and productive workforce. Kelleher says that other companies visited looking for the secret in how Southwest hired, trained, and motivated people. In a 2013 interview, he said it was about paying "personal attention to each of your people." Instead of a "formula," he described the Southwest approach as a "huge mosaic that you're always adding little pieces to make it work." You have to empower employees but also back them up.[81]

However, when you trust employees to make good decisions, sometimes they don't. Like the time Hollywood director Kevin Smith was kicked off a Southwest flight for taking up more than his fair share of space. He got angry, tweeted about his experience, and set off a firestorm of discussion pro and con. An airline representative later acknowledged that "Southwest could have handled this situation differently." In another incident, Southwest received a lot of flak for how a flight attendant dealt with a woman dressed (in the employee's opinion) too provocatively.[82]

Despite these high-profile missteps, Southwest management supported its employees and didn't create more rules. Yes, empowered people will make mistakes. But employees with a sense of ownership will perform at a higher level, too.

In the end, when CEO Gary Kelly says, "Our people are our single greatest strength and most enduring long-term competitive advantage," I tend to believe him. Management actions back this up.

Fair Fares, Without Gimmicks or Tricks

The airline industry pioneered the idea of "revenue management," which essentially means every price is subject to change based on demand, competition, and other factors. The downside of this, of course, is never really knowing if you got the best deal. Sooner or later you're going to end up feeling screwed because a last-minute purchase will be priced outrageously high, but you don't have another choice. Score one for the airlines!

I've always wondered if the geniuses (yes, that was sarcasm) who created these algorithms factored in the loss of trust, along with the ill will generated by a single flight where you felt the airline took advantage of you. On top of that, in recent years airlines seem to be copying banks by layering on fees for bags, changing tickets, and more. Coming soon, a surcharge for breathing air.

The CEO of Ryanair, a low-cost European carrier, is famous for an astonishing array of fees. At one time he proposed a fee to pee.[83] You can't make this stuff up!

Except on Southwest, where the fares are low, simple, and fair. For example, Southwest doesn't charge "change fees"—you just pay the difference between old and new ticket. Frankly, there's no cost rationale for airlines to charge $50, $100, or more to change a ticket, on top of any difference in the ticket itself.

That said, Southwest hasn't avoided fees entirely. For about $25 you can upgrade to a Business Select fare to expedite the airport security process, get early seating and enjoy a free drink. I liked the service and didn't feel like I was being charged for something previously included, which is the sad position of the other airlines.

Increasing Headwinds

Southwest has had a good run, spanning four decades. But that doesn't mean it's immune from competition. In the past ten to fifteen years, key competitors have worked on their cost structure through bankruptcies and consolidation. Meanwhile, Southwest's lower personnel costs are now pretty much gone as its employees have aged and gained seniority. The end of fuel hedges has put Southwest at the mercy of higher fuel costs, just like everyone else.

With fuel and people being two major costs (aircraft being the third, of course), Southwest's cost advantage has eroded and prices have gone up. It's becoming more like a big airline, not an industry disruptor. Meanwhile, JetBlue, Virgin America, and other regional players are winning over customers with a combination of low prices and good experiences.

Still, Southwest has two things not easily copied: 1) loyal customers and 2) friendly and productive employees. I'm betting that Southwest's culture will help it succeed in the years to come, even in the face of a much more challenging competitive environment.

FOOD FOR THOUGHT

- Do employees have real authority to invest in customer relationships?
- Are employees engaged in activities that create customer value?
- Does your company culture put customers or employees first, or balance the two?
- When employees make a mistake, is your first instinct to add to the rule book?
- Are you using technologies to improve access to information, support, and other resources?

Habit 4—Create

Innovation distinguishes between a leader and a follower.
—Steve Jobs

Over the years when I've spoken at conferences and workshops, I've done a group exercise asking for a definition of "customer value." With rare exceptions, attendees usually mention what the customer is buying (revenue), how much money the company makes from the customer's purchase (profit), or customer lifetime value (discounted value of profit stream).

Naturally if you ask customers what they consider valuable, you'll get a completely different answer. At a high level, customers perceive value based on:

- **Function:** the job a product or service performs

- **Experience:** perceptions of interactions with the company

- **Price:** in the context of the function and experience received

In CustomerThink research we have found that customers weigh function about equally with experiences—around 40 percent each. Price gets the remaining 20 percent. Obviously this is a crude measure and varies considerably by industry. Companies need to do good loyalty research (see the "Listen" chapter) to understand what customers really value. Not all value is equally valuable!

The larger point is simply that customers don't see company revenue/ profit generation as value. Some companies forget this. Like banks when they create new service charges out of thin air. Or hotels that use "resort fees" to boost their margins. Or retailers that sell warranty extensions of dubious value to customers.

In the short term these tactics can work (to create value for the company), but when customers feel taken advantage of, they'll seek greener (more valuable) pastures as soon as they can.

Creativity, Invention, and Innovation

Since most every business is constantly updating products and services and launching new ones, it's all too easy for marketers to slap the "innovative" label on just about anything. One point of confusion is that "innovative" is often used as a fancy way of saying something is "creative." Or to refer to a new design "invention."

But these terms are not synonyms. Creativity means looking at the world in novel ways. If you've worked with creative people in music, arts, or business, you know they excel at coming up with ideas. Simplifying a bit here, creativity in a business context means generating ideas.

Ideas may, or may not, get turned into an invention, which means a "unique or novel device, method, composition, or process." Some inventions can be patented to protect the intellectual property rights of the inventor. Steve Jobs didn't invent typefaces, but he is credited with taking the idea of beautiful typography and implementing in a personal computer—the Macintosh. Speaking to a graduating class at Stanford in 2005, he said he got the idea when he dropped out of college and decided to take a class in calligraphy. Ten years later, Jobs designed the first Mac, an *innovation* that came with a selection of fonts unlike anything the PC industry had seen.[84]

Just as not all ideas become inventions, not all inventions become innovations. Because innovation means bringing something new to market that creates economic (or social) value. In other words, you can be as creative as you like and invent lots of new products, but if they aren't commercially successful, it's not really innovative.

Innovation as (New) Value Creation

In a competitive market, customer expectations are constantly being shaped by forces outside your direct control. By direct competitors, certainly. But leaders in a seemingly unrelated industry can also influence customers. When Amazon.com delivered a great book-shopping experience, it raised expectations with customers buying other products in other industries. Experiences using the iPhone influence the design of other products, like cars that are beginning to incorporate new touchscreen designs in the console.

The point is that the customer's perception of value is constantly changing. That's why innovation is a crucial process for any company in a competitive market.

How to be more "innovative" is the subject of countless books, articles, and definitions. Everyone wants to be like Apple, invent the next Post-It, etc. But if you really think about it, innovation is a very simple idea that should be part of any well-run business: create something new, or do something different, to create value for the company.

The new/different part is what innovation experts call "invention." To be truly innovative, the invention needs to create economic value for the inventor (or in some cases, society). Value is the key differentiator, experts say. Still, such a broad concept leads to slapping the "innovative" label on just about anything that creates value:

- Add a new feature to a software product (value = increase sales)

- Improve process management to reduce waste (value = reduced costs)

- Invent a new product (value = penetrate new markets)

That's why "innovation" is a term I've come to love to hate. It's hard to draw a line between what is innovative or not. Is a change big enough to qualify as new or improved? Does it create enough value to have a meaningful impact on the company's performance? Over what time period will the value be created?

For my money, I'll take Jeff Bezos' approach, which is all about leading for the long term at Amazon.com. Sometimes changes in the short term (e.g., the Kindle e-reader sold near cost) don't obviously create value for the company. But it's part of a longer-term approach to create loyal and profitable relationships.

> To be truly innovative, the invention needs to create economic value for the inventor (or in some cases, society).

Bezos has said that "inventing and pioneering requires a willingness to be misunderstood for long periods of time." In the early years of Amazon. com, he was criticized for allowing customer reviews because negative reviews would detract from Amazon's job to "sell things." Bezos held his ground, because: "We don't make money when we sell things. We make money when we help customers make purchase decisions."[85]

Some have questioned customer-centricity as prudent business, because it means do whatever the customer wants, no matter what the consequences. Others position customer-centricity as mainly about focusing on customers (via targeted marketing/selling) to extract more value. Between these two extreme views lies a more practical approach: *A customer-centric business creates value for customers that eventually creates value for the company.*

What does "customer value" mean at your company? Ask around. You'll find the answers enlightening about what really drives your organization's behavior.

Co-created Value

Some argue that for products, the usage experience is a key part of the value proposition. Is this function or experience? In the case of Apple's iPhone, the answer is both—the user experience is very much part of what creates value for the customer. Would the iPhone "function" well if it didn't offer a great experience? No.

Or, take my Weber grill, which I bought to fit a small space on a balcony in my condo. The size, design, quality, and reputation of the Weber brand all factored into my decision to purchase the product. The experience using the grill has been excellent, too.

Using an iPhone or a Weber grill are both examples of co-created value, meaning in part that value is created during the *usage* of the product.

Proponents of this school of thought argue that value doesn't reside in the product or service, but rather in the *experience* of using that product or service.

A related concept is service-dominant logic, which essentially argues that *everything* is a service. All firms are service firms, and the "customer is always a co-creator of value."[86]

Really? I'm suspicious of "always," especially when it comes to a discussion about business–customer relationships. There are exceptions to any rule. While I agree that experiences and customer–company collaboration are immensely important, they don't account for all forms of customer value.

For example, when I buy a shovel and store it in the garage for future use, part of the "value" comes from knowing that it will be available for future use. A luxury car gives me a good feeling (another form of value) even when it's parked and out of sight. Even though rarely used, insurance policies give me peace of mind. In none of these cases did I participate in the value creation via collaborative development or usage.

Which Comes First, Ideas or Needs?

The progression from ideas to inventions to innovation makes logical sense. And ideas are plentiful. Perhaps too plentiful. In recent years social media and ideation tools have been used to generate ideas even faster. Visit My Starbucks Idea (mystarbucksidea.force.com) and you'll see thousands of ideas for new products, experiences, and even community involvement. As of this writing, only a few are moving forward, such as nonsmoking patios, healthier food options, and soft pretzels.

Many companies have implemented a similar approach for collaborative idea generation—part of the open innovation movement—including Dell, Sara Lee, IBM, and P&G. Sophisticated ideation tools can help users submit ideas and manage voting and ranking activities to find the most popular. Ideas can also be mined from social media, including Facebook, Twitter, blogs, and community forums.[87]

While stimulating or mining ideas may lead to innovation, it's backward and inefficient, according to Tony Ulwick of Strategyn, an innovation consulting firm. Starting with ideas first is a "guessing game" because companies "hope that the idea will be in a market that's big enough to make sense for them to pursue." He instead advocates for "outcome-driven innovation," which starts with a market big enough to pursue and then strives to find unmet needs in that market.

> The goal is really to pick the correct market, discover where to focus in that market, see if it's worth focusing on creating a solution in that market, and once all those questions are asked, then come up with a solution that addresses the unmet needs in the market.

A case in point is the development of the Bosch CS20 circular saw. Bosch had hundreds of ideas, but couldn't figure out which ones to pursue in a market that seemed saturated. Through painstaking research they identified a segment with important but unmet needs, which indicates "where customers are struggling to get the job done better." Ulwick said that Bosch put fourteen different features on the CS20 saw to meet those needs at a competitive price, and it became their fastest-growing product in North American history.[88]

Delight, by Design. Innovation Sets Intuit Apart

Let's admit it. Innovation is cool. What company wouldn't like to appear on one of those "most innovative" lists? So what's the problem? Just brainstorm some new ideas, pick the best one, take it to market, and let the good times roll. Let's all go innovate!

Obviously, innovation is not quite that simple. Else why would Amazon.com sell *fifty-seven thousand* books and Google give you *280 million hits* on the subject?

Innovation is critical for long-term survival. Competitors are hell-bent to take away your customers. Technology creates new opportunities that can transform industries. And customers? They have problems you haven't solved. Yet.

Creative Destruction

Most companies focus on fixing problems and refining what they're already doing. That's all well and good, but customer-centric leaders also strive to create new products and services for *unmet* customer needs.

One of the best in the world at this is software maker Intuit, which sells solutions for mundane tasks like accounting, personal finances, and paying taxes—and somehow makes it exciting! The company booked over $4 billion in 2012 and has been growing 10 percent compounded per year for the past five years. During that period, its stock price doubled while Microsoft (a key rival) and the S&P 500 stock index increased only 20 percent.[89]

Speaking at a conference in 2011, Roy Rosin, vice president of innovation at Intuit, explained how Quicken Health Expense Tracker was inspired by one family's challenges dealing with $1 million (that's right, *million*) in medical bills. Intuit launched the product in 2004 and then kept enhancing it for five years, improving its Net Promoter Score (a measure of customer loyalty) from terrible (-19) to awesome (+77). By early 2011 Rosin said the software was being used by three million patients and thirty-three thousand doctors.[90]

This is a wonderful case study of a new solution being launched based on real customer insight (new product innovation) and then continuously improved (incremental innovation) to reach its full potential. A success story, right?

Not exactly. Intuit shut down Health Expense Tracker in 2012 because they found a "greater need and opportunity for us to improve the way patients interact with their healthcare providers online." That solution was Health Patient Portal (healthcare.intuit.com/portal/), which amassed *seven million subscribers* by June 2013. Intuit CEO Brad Smith explained matter-of-factly the firm's philosophy in a July 2012 interview: "If the customer is adopting it we double down. If not we shut it down."[91]

Think about this. Intuit solved a key customer problem. Improved the software over five years. And then killed it—a compelling example of a company *doing its own creative destruction* before competitors can do it for them! How many companies are littered with products on life support because leaders don't have the guts to stop and move on to better solutions?

"Could We Do More?"

This process didn't happen by accident. One of Intuit's core values is "Innovate and Improve," defined as:

> We innovate to drive growth, and continuously improve everything we do. We move with speed and agility, and embrace change. We have the courage to take risks, and grow by learning from our successes and failures.[92]

Company leaders really do encourage risk-taking. Take, for example, the Free Tax Advice service (turbotax.intuit.com/tax-answers), which, as the name implies, gives tax advice. For free. Seriously?

Surely Intuit would only make this available to paying customers. Or set up a premium subscription. You can't just give this away, right? Well, yes they can, and did.

The idea came from observing that customers looked to TurboTax as a source for answers on how to use the software but not for tax advice. This raised the question, according to product manager Katie Hanson, "Could we do more?" With support from an aggressive general manager, they decided to market it as "we give tax advice" with no use of an Intuit product required.

Intuit Design for Delight

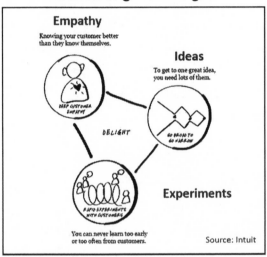

Source: Intuit

This service, along with many other solutions, is the result of Intuit's Design for Delight approach to innovation. It was initiated in 2007 when founder Scott Cook realized the company wasn't wowing customers. The company adopted Net Promoter Score in 2004 but found it mainly helped fix problems. That cut the percentage of "defectors" but did little to increase "promoters"—those answering "nine" or "ten" on the scale of likelihood to recommend. Cook realized he had to focus the entire organization on innovation, in contrast to the Steve Jobs model with a visionary calling the shots from the top.[93]

Since the tax advice service involved hiring hundreds of agents, it was very risky. But Intuit believed it would increase customer loyalty and drive new product sales. Leaders were willing to take a risk to *add value* to existing customers and potential customers. If this strategy stops working and a better approach appears, they won't be afraid to move on.

My too-good-to-be-true warning light flashing, I decided to try the service with a real tax question. After entering it into the online form, I got a list of possible answers from their online knowledgebase, followed by options to contact Intuit through its TurboTax community, online chat, and phone.

Yes, it really was delightful. If you're already a TurboTax customer, this service will keep you one for life. If not, the next time you're in the market for tax software, you'll be buying from Intuit.

Making Creating Value a Habit

While innovation requires creativity, it shouldn't be like catching lightning in a bottle. Great companies manage innovation as a repeatable process or organizational habit. Leaders like Intuit make it part of the culture. Here are some quick words of advice:

- **Make it OK to fail.** In fact, maybe you should *celebrate* failure, because without failure there is no innovation. People won't try something risky otherwise. Leaders must set the tone, recognize winners, and not punish those who don't succeed every time.

- **Track progress with appropriate metrics.** Innovation should not be a popularity contest or a marketing slogan. You need objective evidence of progress. Innovation expert Robert Brands recommends using a combination of leading (e.g., number of ideas generated, patents filed) and lagging (e.g., new product sales as percentage of total, number of patents issued) success measures.

- **Start with customer needs.** There's a place for truly disruptive technologies and ideas that can transform an industry. But these are few and far between. A Cooper-Edgett Ideation Study found Voice of Customer methods the most popular and effective, including customer visit teams, customer focus groups for problem detection, and lead-user analysis.[94]

Fixing problems isn't enough. In the end, it's up to business leaders to make innovation a priority and implement sustaining processes and reward systems.

How Weber and Home Depot Earned My Business

With our son off to college, my wife and I downsized into a condo and gave away our large backyard barbeque grill. We were in the market for a new grill. Here's how Weber and Home Depot won my business with the right product and experience.

Like most consumers these days, I started with a search on Google. Wow, "small barbeque grill" got over four million hits! Undaunted, I eventually checked out some of the major brands—including Char Broil and Weber—and retailers that I trusted—like Amazon.com, Home Depot, and Lowes.

In the process, I found several grills that could work, but it was hard to envision how they would fit on our small balcony. I visited the local Home Depot to check out what they had in stock and see the dimensions.

Back online, I started narrowing down my options. Checking reviews was a key part of making a decision. It wasn't as simple as which grill got the higher rating. What really helped was the discussion of pros and cons. One Char Broil model I liked, but the reviews about a new "infrared" heating approach got mixed reviews. Even after seeing that specific grill in the store, I couldn't quite figure out how this made grilling better and decided to stick with a regular gas grill.

Weber kept popping up, and this is where things got interesting. I never actually saw the Weber grill I wanted in person. But the photos and information on the retailer and manufacturer websites, along with customer comments, sold me on the Weber Q 300.

The price was the same everywhere I checked. The main difference was shipping costs and/or pickup convenience. Lowes had a very expensive shipping option; Amazon and Home Depot were a bit lower. But I really didn't want to pay (or wait) for shipping when there were stores nearby.

I decided to buy the grill online at www.homedepot.com and pick it up at a local store. The purchasing process was easy, almost as nice as Amazon.com. I got the usual confirmation messages, along with a promise that I'd get email and text alerts when the grill was available for pickup.

Unfortunately, I never got either alert. Checking online, I found the grill was ready and went to Home Depot to pick it up. There the process was smooth—a clerk took my paperwork, got the grill from the back, and helped me take it to my car.

Standing with this huge box at the back of my economy car, I realized it would never fit. So right there the Home Depot guy and I unpacked the grill so I could fit the components into my car. Then, after saying he really wasn't supposed to, he took away the packing material with a smile, saving me the disposal hassle when I got home.

After getting it home, the grill was easy to put together. Clear instructions, wonderful design, and only a couple of expletives when I banged a finger. And, yes, the grill does a great job grilling Bob's Famous Salmon!

Lessons Learned

These days there's a lot of talk about customer experience and a fair amount of hyperbole that it's the only thing that matters. Well, in this case the *product* was far and away the most important factor. Weber *earned my business with its innovative design.* The grill I selected had a unique combination of size and style that appealed to me.

In other words, Weber totally nailed the "job to be done" for me. Instead of thinking of market segments based on demographics or psychographics, marketers design products to perform functional, emotional, and social "jobs."[95] In my case, the functional (size to fit my space, quality grill) and emotional (a good-looking design) jobs were most important.

That said, when a product is available through multiple channels, *the retailer that provides the best experience will get the order.* In this case, Home Depot's integration of online and offline shopping was valuable to me. Other points to consider:

- **Brand does matter.** Whether it's entirely fair or not, I was drawn to major brands that I had used or was familiar with. It's possible I missed a better grill in the process.

- **Reviews influenced my decision.** I didn't ask any personal friends, but the online reviews were instrumental in making my decision from a short list of possibilities.

- **The purchasing location was a more subtle consideration.** I like Amazon.com and wouldn't give it a second thought for books and electronics. But for this purchase it just seemed to make more sense to buy from a home retailer.

- **Home Depot integrated clicks, bricks, and people.** While it wasn't flawless, the retailer did a great job overall supporting my buying process online, in the store, and with their staff.

- **A little something extra made it memorable.** The final "touch-point" where I got some extra help with the box in the parking lot was the cherry on top.

Shopper Psychology: Why CEO Ron Johnson Failed at JC Penney

Several years ago, my first visit to an Apple store was to buy an iPod for my son. Amazing experience. The store had a clean and open design, and the staff was really helpful. When I was ready to buy, I realized something was missing. The checkout line!

Instead of a row of registers at the front, the staffer just pulled out a scanner from underneath a table, charged my credit card, printed a receipt, and we were on our way.

Much of the credit for that store design goes to Ron Johnson, Apple's former senior VP of retail operations. Johnson joined Apple in 2000 after earning his retail stripes at Target and Mervyns. The Apple store design eventually became the biggest success story in retail: twice as productive as Tiffany and *seven times* the median of the top twenty retailers.[96]

Of course, Apple's stores wouldn't have been such a huge hit without massively popular products such as the iPod, iPhone, and iPad. (That will turn out to be an important issue, as you read on.)

Johnson was hired to reprise his Apple success at a more conventional retailer—JC Penney (JCP). Prior to his arrival, I would summarize the retailer's pricing strategy as: "If you didn't buy this on sale, you're an idiot!" Appointed the CEO in November 2011, Johnson set a new course for the struggling retailer, including fresh store designs and everyday low prices. He hired new executives and told Wall Street the transformation could take four years.

Then Q1 2012 results came in, and it was ugly. Analysts started questioning the strategy, and JCP made some adjustments to its pricing. While everyday low prices would still be the core, JCP added selected specials on seasonal items. When the next quarter results were posted, they were still dismal. The company lost $147 million and said it wouldn't meet its yearly profit forecast.

Staying the Course

Despite these early setbacks, Johnson vowed to stay the course. At the time, I applauded him (and his board of directors) for not bowing to the short-term interests of Wall Street. After all, when Apple launched the innovative retail store design, including the now-famous Genius Bar, most people forget that it wasn't an instant success. In an interview, Johnson said, "It takes courage to go the full distance."

> You know, when we launched the Genius Bar years ago, nobody came. I mean literally after a year and a half, a lot of people at Apple said why don't you close that down? We had to put in Evian bottles of water in refrigerators to get people to spend time at the

bar. But we stuck with it, and today, you look at that Genius Bar. Could you imagine an Apple store without a Genius Bar? Could you imagine owning an iPhone without having a place to stop by and get that repaired or restored or fixed? You couldn't.[97]

I rooted for Johnson because this sort of courage is all too rare. JCP's challenge, though, is quite a bit different from Apple's. First, Apple had killer products. Second, it had a blank sheet to create a new technology retail experience, focused on Apple's products.

JCP, on the other hand, sells a multitude of products that can be bought elsewhere—like Macy's, Kohl's, and more. And JCP has trained its customers to expect price promotions. Some people love getting things on sale, even though oftentimes it's just an illusion. Here's an example from a happy JCP shopper in 2010, who loves getting deals: "So I think you now see why I love shopping at JCP. Designer brands, sales, coupons, and free gift certificates. All the elements a bargainista loves…"[98]

The problem is that changing customer expectations, and habits, takes time. "Bargainistas" are going to shop elsewhere, and JCP would need to win customers away from other retailers with a superior experience, not just promotions.

Under Johnson's leadership, the marketing strategy changed dramatically. One Sunday in our local paper were promotional inserts from the usual retailers. Macy's front page screamed "20%-60% OFF STOREWIDE." Kohl's promoted 35 to 50 percent off early bird specials on Saturday, plus additional discounts for using a Kohl's credit card. Both had the usual clutter of ads and product promotions inside.

By contrast, JCP's insert was like a catalog. A crisp design consistent with Johnson's new direction. The front page said simply "back-to-school favorites" with a selection of featured products inside showing their everyday low prices, one product per page. Only the last of the twenty-four pages promoted clearance items, without discount percentages.

What Went Wrong?

Despite proclamations of support from JCP's board, after losing $4 billion in revenue and a precipitous drop in stock price, Johnson was fired less than eighteen months into a turnaround that he said would take four years. What happened?

Some blamed the everyday low pricing strategy, which Johnson believed to be more honest. In a January 2012 *Fast Company* interview he said, "Why do they lie to the customer about the regular price? Why do they make up a regular price to sell it on sale? I don't understand being dishonest about pricing."[99]

Retail consultant Dale Furtwengler argued that JCP's everyday pricing didn't work because the retailer lacked a clear brand promise and had yet to modernize new stores and offer unique brands. There needs to a "congruency between the four elements of a pricing strategy—brand promise, marketing messages, sales scripts, and pricing."[100]

What was the JCP brand promise that Johnson was trying to recreate? Good question. My take is that he wanted to emulate the "cheap chic" brand that he helped create at Target. Personally I like the idea of "fair and square pricing," but in the rough and tumble world of retail, a lot of people are hooked on "sales" and JCP's competitors are happy to oblige. Adding private label brands takes time, but without unique goods to sell, JCP will continue to sell brands available elsewhere.

One thing both supporters and detractors agree on—Johnson's strategy was a huge gamble. In my view, to succeed, Johnson had to do four difficult things simultaneously:

- Convince current JCP shoppers that everyday low pricing is better than constant deals,

- Implement new store designs with more unique, upscale products,

- Attract new shoppers to try the new, improved JCP, and

- Convince Wall Street, his board, and the employees to keep the faith.

To put it simply: Johnson failed because *JCP is not Apple*. However, it's also true that his board didn't back him for the time required. At Amazon.com, its board gave Jeff Bezos latitude to build Amazon into what it is today, without worrying about short-term results.

As many have pointed out, perhaps Johnson tried to do too much, too quickly. As one illustration of why sales were so bad, I spoke with a long-time JCP shopper who was turned off by some of the changes. Some of her favorite clothing was ditched in favor of more fashionable clothing lines, and loud disco-pop music "drove her crazy."

It seemed Johnson wanted to attract a different kind of shopper—younger, more fashion conscious, less driven by deals. But he didn't factor in the time required to remake a brand. Upsetting your current customers, by contrast, can be done remarkably fast.

Shopper Psychology: Discounts Are Value

It's always been interesting to me how little attention price gets in discussions about customer loyalty. Pricing is the "elephant in the room." Yes, companies should work hard to innovate in products and experiences and not fall into a commodity trap of selling solely on (low) price.

But there is a human side to pricing that can't be ignored. A *New York Times* article chalked up Johnson's failure to a poor understanding of shopper psychology. Some shoppers actually enjoy getting discounts even when the end price is about the same as "everyday low prices."[101]

Shoppers need cues to figure out what something is worth. A discount off an inflated list price is a cue many can't resist, because they think they're getting a deal based on the reference point provided by the higher, presale price. Social scientists refer to this phenomenon as "anchoring," and it applies to all sorts of consumer behavior and expectations. Without the list price anchor, consumers have trouble determining whether the store is actually giving them a good price.[102]

Most of the discussion around customer value is about differentiating products and services or in creating great experiences. But most of us like getting deals. Only a few brands like Apple can succeed with a "take it or leave it" pricing strategy. JCP is not one of those brands.

Lessons Learned

In the early goings post-Johnson, it appears that JCP will scale back many of Johnson's changes. Discounting is back, and it's unclear whether store upgrades will be continued. Still, the short and tumultuous Johnson tenure illustrated a few key points for innovators:

- **Be ready to go the distance.** Christopher Columbus said, "You can never cross the ocean unless you have the courage to lose sight of the shore." I would add that you also need the courage to not turn back when the going gets rough.

- **If you can't execute, it's just an idea.** Remember, innovation must create value for the customer and the company. We'll never know if Johnson's ideas would have worked, because he attempted too many changes at the same time.

- **Pricing does matter.** A price-only strategy won't work unless you have the economic power of companies like Walmart. For most everyone else, pricing is a critical part of the value package.

How Amazon Wins: Innovation, Low Prices, and Free Cash Flow

In 2005 CustomerThink gave Amazon.com a customer-centric leadership award. In an acceptance letter, Craig Berman, Amazon's director of platform and technology communications, said:

> It is simply in our DNA to approach our business by starting with the customer and working backward, and for the past ten years we have stayed laser-focused on this core principle.

In the following years, Amazon.com has shown that customer-centricity is more than a slogan. The company keeps innovating to serve existing customers by expanding what it sells and how consumers access its content (e.g., Kindle). But it has also been a pioneer into new markets like cloud computing with Amazon Web Services.

Without Amazon, we wouldn't hear terms like "showrooming," which terrifies traditional retailers. Using mobile phones, shoppers can visit a retail store to inspect merchandise, then shop for the best price online. Retailers think this is unfair because they have invested in the store experience but don't get the order.

But they have other reasons to be worried. Amazon has been quietly testing its Amazon Fresh grocery service in Seattle. According to an article in the *San Francisco Chronicle*, Bezos may create new fulfillment centers in major US cities to handle perishable items. The author opines that it wouldn't take much to deliver other products from local centers within twenty-four hours.

Target and Walmart, Hello. Are You Paying Attention?

For all the talk about innovation, customer-centricity, and a great online experience, what underpins Amazon.com's success is simply this: Low Prices. That's right, low prices. Seriously, would you pay more for the convenience of shopping online? I doubt it.

> Bezos has proven that you can offer popular products at a low price and do so packaged in a great shopping experience.

However, in the real world, low prices are often associated with a bad experience. While there are exceptions like Southwest Airlines, the conventional wisdom is that there's a tradeoff between price and customer experience. For brick-and-mortar retailers, that may be true, because it costs real money to run a store, train staff, etc. Just ask Best Buy, which has been struggling to find its way as electronics buyers shift online. However, in the online world where Amazon reigns supreme, economics work a bit differently. Bezos has proven that you can offer popular products at a low price and do so packaged in a great shopping experience.

In the early days, Wall Street analysts told Amazon CEO Jeff Bezos he needed to increase prices to get his margins up. He didn't listen. Instead, he challenged his leadership team to cut their cost of operation so they could continue to offer the best deal to consumers.

Frankly, the more I hear about Amazon's strategy, the more it sounds like Costco or Walmart. Except Bezos doesn't have to sacrifice the customer experience in exchange for low prices.

Of course, we've all seen too-good-to-be-true business models that were not sustainable. Sooner or later, you have to pay your bills. Bezos is more concerned with cash flow than making money because he believes the opportunity offered by the Internet, and by e-commerce, is huge and largely untapped. He's prepared to cut prices to the bone and add all those freebies to cultivate customer loyalty and increase sales. Then he reinvests it all in more low prices and further expansion, creating additional customer loyalty.[103]

How else can you explain all the freebies you get with Amazon Prime?

FOOD FOR THOUGHT

- Does your organization have a balanced perspective on value from and for customers?
- How do your partners contribute to customer value creation?
- Are you realistic about the role that pricing plays in customer decision-making?
- Is innovation part of your corporate culture or just a job for research and development?
- How many radically new solutions do you introduce compared to incremental improvements?

Habit 5—Delight

The key is to set realistic customer expectations,
and then not to just meet them, but to exceed them—
preferably in unexpected and helpful ways.
—Richard Branson

One day I took my mother to a Wells Fargo branch office to take care of three different transactions: getting a credit card reactivated, depositing coins, and ordering checks. The coins required a visit, but the other two transactions could have been done by phone or maybe online. I hoped one visit to a local branch would be easier, but deep down I feared it wouldn't.

Frankly, I expected we'd be shuttled around the branch to different people to take care of each transaction. Or, worse, told to use the phone to call the credit card support number directly.

Instead, it turned into a quick and—dare I say it—*delightful* experience. Because when we entered the branch, a banker warmly greeted us and asked how he could help. After learning what my mother wanted to do, he invited us to sit down at his desk and then took care of everything:

1. Called the credit card division of Wells Fargo to activate a credit card,

2. Took the coins to the teller to make the deposit and returned with a receipt, and

3. Ordered new checks.

Before inviting us to sit down, the banker didn't know us or how much money we had at Wells Fargo. Or whether I was influential on social media. CRM advocates might say that the banker's personal (read: expensive) effort could have been misplaced, because the banker didn't know our lifetime value. One of the basic tenets of CRM is to invest more resources in valuable customers.

CEM proponents would be concerned for different reasons. After we finished, he didn't give us a satisfaction survey or ask if we would recommend Wells Fargo to our friends and family. Instead, he said we were welcome to have a cookie before leaving. So we did!

The *personal* touch by this banker is what made our visit both efficient and delightful. Think about what your frontline people are doing when approached by customers. Are they just traffic cops for your service channels—the human equivalent of an IVR? Or will they take ownership and add value personally?

Keep Trying to Delight Your Customers

In the 2010 *Harvard Business Review* (*HBR*) article "Stop Trying to Delight Your Customers," authors from the Corporate Executive Board (CEB) argue that consumers are more inclined to punish bad service than to reward delightful service. Therefore, companies should focus on delivering the basics, which is more likely to drive loyalty.[104]

Really? The title of the article is provocative and the authors make a number of great points. But if you take their advice literally, you'll lose a great opportunity to create genuine customer loyalty.

Let's start with what the CEB study got right. If your customers are calling to get a problem solved, satisfying that request quickly and easily *is* very important. If you don't, customers will be dissatisfied, and that leads to defection and negative word of mouth.

But the authors take that point and extrapolate too far, implying that:

- Customer service transactions are the only opportunity to create true loyalty.

- Placating customers after a failure is the same as creating delight.

- Companies should adopt Customer Effort Score (CES) as a general-purpose loyalty metric.

Satisfiers versus Delighters

It's true that overachieving on basic customer service (or other "hygiene" expectations) is usually a waste of company resources; it doesn't

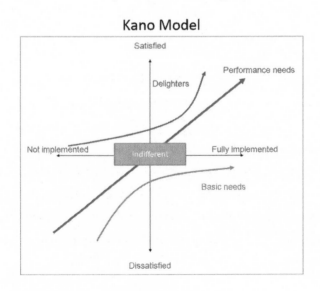

Kano Model

move the needle to create positive customer loyalty. This insight is hardly new; it is based on the Kano model and other related research on drivers of satisfaction and loyalty.

Here are a few examples to illustrate my point:

- If you go to a bank to use the ATM and it doesn't work, you'll be unhappy and more likely to switch banks if it keeps occurring. Is it worth trying to delight customer when they just want to withdraw cash and be on their way? Probably not. Now ATMs are viewed as a basic need, with little opportunity to delight, only to disappoint (if they don't work).

- When you stay at a hotel, you expect your room to be clean. What if the hotel made it so clean you could use it for surgical procedures? Again, a waste of resources. A clean room is enough; the hotel should focus its resources on other areas to delight you. Like DoubleTree, which gives away sixty thousand chocolate chip cookies every day. An unexpected treat is more likely to create a positive impression, but won't harm customer satisfaction if it's missing.

- And then there's the contact center, which was the focus of the CEB study. Does trying to delight the customer in basic service interactions pay off in positive loyalty? Again, probably not for the average company struggling to get the basics right. Still, Zappos has demonstrated that with the right people, customer service calls can still be a loyalty-building experience. Read on for a personal story on why I bet on the Zappos culture to deal with an unhappy shopper.

Delighting or Placating Customers?

Delight literally means a combination of surprise and joy. To create delight with the customer, you need to do more than what's expected. However, it's not easy to translate delight into a business practice. Measuring delight is also tricky. Getting a "totally satisfied" or "very likely to recommend" rating is not the same as exceeding expectations, according to Howard Lax of GfK Customer Loyalty.

The CEB study found that eighty-nine of one hundred customer service heads wanted to exceed customer expectations with extras like "offering a refund, a free product, or a free service such as expedited shipping." Yet 84 percent of customers *didn't* feel their expectations were exceeded. As a result, customers were "only marginally more loyal than simply meeting their needs."

In my view, these are examples of *placating* customers, not delighting them. Consumers get offered extras when the company has screwed up. Personally, I don't want to make customer service calls, but if I have to, I want my problem solved pronto. Any extras aren't really "exceeding my expectations," *they are making up for the fact that my expectations weren't met.*

If you don't exceed expectations (as customers perceive it), you're not actually delighting customers, are you? And, therefore, it's hardly surprising that there's little loyalty impact.

What Really Drives Loyalty?

The CEB study authors start with service interactions then extrapolate to create a new loyalty metric called Customer Effort Score (CES), a measure of ease of doing business. That's backward.

Let's remember that service interactions with the contact center are just one part of the total customer experience. Other experiences (e.g., in marketing, selling, and purchasing) also matter. And so does the quality, usability, and "fit" of the core product/service. Recall that in the "Listen" chapter, I advise companies to do the research to find both drivers of dissatisfaction (if you don't meet expectations) and delight (when you exceed expectations).

In the Ipsos Loyalty white paper "The Role of Customer Delight in Achieving Loyalty" you'll find a great discussion of the role of alleviating pain versus creating true delight. Clear communications and solving problems in one call/visit are both of high importance on "curing pain," yet have low impact on creating delight. Providing the "right amount of information and assistance" has the opposite effect.[105]

Similarly, GfK Customer Loyalty found in a 2011 retail banking study that "knows your history" is a driver of dissatisfaction but *not* a loyalty driver. In other words, it's a "hygiene" expectation—a bank gets no credit for knowing its customers' history, only blame when it doesn't. But, "appreciates your business" can drive both dissatisfaction *and* loyalty. And, "helps you be smart about money" is not a basic expectation, so it's a great opportunity for banks to delight customers. There's no downside if they don't (yet).

Commenting on the CEB study, Howard Lax of GfK Customer Loyalty says:

> Making things "easy" isn't the same as instilling loyalty. Their point seems to be to forget about loyalty, just reduce the barriers to doing business with your firm. I don't think this is enough to create stickiness; it just seems to (partially) address the problem side of the equation. Basically, they treat everything as a "hygiene" factor. This might make sense when thinking about sending out statements (not much opportunity to WOW folks there), but seems to miss the larger point.

In a comment on his *HBR* article, Matt Dixon says the problem is that "companies focus their customer service strategies and resources on exceeding expectations (providing those moments of 'wow') when they struggle to simply meet expectations a huge percentage of the time." The majority of customers (roughly six out of ten) experience frustrations during routine service interactions, such as "callbacks, repeating information, transfers, channel switching, etc."

Dixon is absolutely right—this is the sand in the gears of the service experience that should be removed. In CustomerThink's US consumer study, I found that "touchpoint amnesia" (company forgetting customer information from one touchpoint to the next) had a dramatic negative impact on customer loyalty and purchase propensity. That is just one example of a core service experience problem that should be fixed.

Strive for Real Delight, Not Appeasement

If you really understand what the CEB study found, the headline should read as "Stop Placating Your Customers, Get It Right the First Time." Bill Price, author of *The Best Service Is No Service*, pioneered a rigorous approach at Amazon.com to finding and fixing the reasons that customers needed service. While Amazon.com made accommodations for customers when it failed to meet expectations, it was (and still is) obsessed with figuring out how to *stop making the same mistakes*!

The *HBR* article title is misleadingly broad, and the CES loyalty metric seems contrived to measure just one element of the customer experience. But the CEB authors' message to focus on the basics is important, especially in customer service experiences.

My take is that companies need to work on two fronts continuously:

- **Systematically root out the causes of customer pain.** This will reduce dissatisfaction and defection, a worthwhile goal in most any business.

- **Figure out how to truly delight customers on things that matter.** At least, if you aspire to be a company that leads your industry.

Delight is in fact a critical strategy to differentiate and build real customer loyalty. Just be sure to invest in areas where it will pay off. In the meantime, stop making mistakes that annoy your customers!

People: The Secret Sauce in Delightful Experiences

There is a tremendous opportunity to innovate the customer experience with digital or social technology. One of my favorite examples is Tesco's virtual subway store in South Korea. Shoppers see a virtual display in the subway, order by mobile phone, and the store delivers![106]

Really cool stuff. However, time and time again, when I ask people to recall a "memorable experience" they rarely speak about technology. After the initial rush of excitement, technology fades into the background—like the ATM that always works or easy-to-use online banking.

People are what customers talk about most often. This was confirmed for me once again at a 2012 Chief Customer Officer Forum organized by Bill Price of Driva Solutions. In a group exercise, I asked executives to think about recent "memorable" experiences, good or bad. Out of twenty people, twelve recounted positive experiences and the rest were negative. About 80 percent of these memorable interactions were about how an employee handled a situation. Here's a sample:

- A United Airlines frequent flyer was upgraded to first class and was told they would serve a meal. After getting on board the flight, he found that wasn't true. The flight attendant wasn't empathetic and said the passenger could buy a meal from coach.

My take: This was a process failure that could have been recovered from by just giving the passenger a meal from coach. Why wasn't the flight attendant *empowered* to do so?

- During routine car maintenance an Infinity owner was informed that her car had a small ding. She declined to spend the one hundred dollars to fix it. The dealer fixed it anyway, for free!

My take: This was a small repair that didn't cost the dealer much (a few minutes to pull out the dent) yet earned a lot in customer loyalty. Great example of "marketing lagniappe" (a little something extra).

- A customer of a pool and spa company absolutely hated the company due to lousy service. Yet he shopped there anyway because it was the only convenient store that carried the products he needed. During his last visit he was pleasantly surprised to find a delightful service experience because the store had hired a new manager.

My take: A classic story of a "trapped" customer who was not really loyal. *Leadership* turned things around, not products or price. How much do you think positive word of mouth will be worth to that store?

- A Saks customer bought a new dress for an important event. After getting it home, she found the security device still attached. She called Saks; they sent someone over immediately and removed it.

My take: It's a good thing that the United Airlines flight attendant didn't get that call! ("Could you drive back to the store and, oh, be sure to bring your receipt, three forms of ID, and $20 as a service fee to pay us to remove the tag.")

- A Cuisinart owner had a problem with the product and finally sent it in for repairs after several calls. Three weeks later, no replacement, no update. Called for a status and was told it would be *another* three to four weeks. Now using a competing product and wouldn't recommend Cuisinart to others.

My take: A poorly designed service process that left the customer in the dark. Even high-quality "premium" products have alternatives. Why didn't Cuisinart give a replacement order a higher priority? Send an automated email with estimated ship date? Have a clue?

- A Bank of America customer was amazed when a rep offered to help her reduce the number of accounts and eliminate monthly charges. This was a personal touch she didn't receive at a small hometown bank.

My take: Great example that big doesn't have to mean impersonal. Why don't more companies help their customers "rightsize" their spending, instead of letting customers discover that the best deals go to new customers? Companies are training customers to threaten to quit, because that's how you get a fair deal.

To be sure, some of these incidents could have been avoided entirely because, as Price likes to say, "the best service is no service." But problems occur in even the best-run companies, so service experiences are a great opportunity to stand out.

The results of this exercise were remarkably consistent with other meetings I've conducted over the years. A major 2006 CustomerThink research study found a fifty-fifty split of positive/negative experiences, where people-related factors accounted for about *70 percent of memorable experiences.*

In that study we also identified these top five attributes of companies that delivered "consistently excellent customer experiences":

1. Well-trained and helpful employees

2. Excellent customer service

3. High-quality goods and services

4. Friendly and caring employees

5. Personal attention, reward for loyalty

Review this list and it's clear why people are a critical part of any strategy to delight customers.

Betting $100 on the Zappos Culture

At an executive event in Chicago in 2011, I spoke about Zappos as an example of a customer-centric company that really worked hard to delight its customers when they called or connected on social networks.

I asked the audience if there were any Zappos customers, and the majority raised their hands. Then I asked if anyone had ever had a *bad* experience with Zappos. A marketing executive raised his hand and said he wasn't happy with Zappos' ads following him around online after he visited the site. (Note: This is called "retargeting," which marketers find can dramatically increase the effectiveness of banner ads.)

Without really thinking about it, I promised him that if he called Zappos to discuss the issue, he'd be happy with the way they responded. To show that I was serious, I wagered $100 and gave him my business card. Here's what happened, according to the email he sent to Zappos CEO Tony Hsieh (copying me):

I attended a power breakfast at the Ritz-Carlton last week hosted by CustomerThink CEO Bob Thompson. He asked the audience if anyone had a bad customer experience with Zappos and I was the only person in the audience who raised their hand. Truth be told, I have never been a customer and this was the explanation I gave Bob and the audience.

About a year ago, I was looking for a pair of Pumas online and searched your site. For weeks afterward, Zappos ads followed me around to nearly every site I visited, which kind of creeped me out. Creepier still, all the ads displayed Pumas exclusively. I qualified my statement with the fact that all my female friends rave about their customer experience with Zappos. In the end, I was reticent about visiting your site again and purchased my Pumas from a DSW retail store here in Chicago.

Bob then handed me his business card and told everyone he would send me $100 if I contacted customer service and wasn't satisfied with the experience. Well, it doesn't appear that I will be collecting any money from Bob, copied here. Anita, my rep today, was empathetic, ebullient, and an all-around cheerful person. She also gave me your email address (amazing!), took mine, and said she'd look into this matter and get back to me. I can't ask for more than that. Never once did I feel rushed, which is rare in a call center environment.

I'm not a gambling man. When I go to Las Vegas, I never put so much as a quarter in a slot machine or play blackjack or anything else. Why did I wager $100 on Zappos' customer service?

Because when I visited Zappos headquarters in 2009 I saw firsthand that the culture really is different. The vast majority of Zappos revenue is booked online. But when someone does call for help on an order or to deal with a problem, Zappos wants the service experience to be fantastic. According to Zappos.com, they don't view customer service as a "department."

> We've been asked by a lot of people how we've grown so quickly, and the answer is actually really simple… We've aligned the entire organization around one mission: to provide the best customer service possible. Internally, we call this our WOW philosophy.[107]

Zappos invests in systems, for sure. But the real secret is their culture and the people they hire. A bit quirky (piercings and tattoos are plentiful), but all sharing a passion for serving customers. Instead of "agents" or "service reps," Zappos calls call center agents "customer loyalty representatives." Their key measurement is customer satisfaction, not average handle time or some other efficiency metric.

In my view, Zappos does a brilliant job of putting it all together. Great people backed by strong systems and processes and driven by a culture that is passionate about delivering delightful customer experiences. All thanks to Tony Hsieh's leadership. That's why I wagered $100 without any concern. In my mind, it was a sure thing!

1001 Ways to Delight

I believe that cost is used too often as an excuse for a lack of creativity and leadership. Still, exceeding expectations means doing more, which must cost something, right? Maybe, maybe not.

Are you struggling to delight customers without breaking the budget? Then pick up a copy of *What's Your Purple Goldfish?* by Stan Phelps. The book contains crowd-sourced examples of "marketing lagniappe," which means: "Any time a business goes above and beyond to provide a 'little something extra' for a customer. It's that unexpected surprise that's thrown in for good measure." The Purple Goldfish Project home page offers these examples to get you warmed up to the idea:

- Southwest Airlines: Grab your bag…it's on. Southwest doesn't charge for bags.

- TD Bank: TD Bank has a penny arcade in their lobby, a free service to all who want to exchange coins

- Five Guys Burgers and Fries: Free peanuts while you wait and extra fries with your order (lots of them)

- Stew Leonard's: Buy $100 or more of groceries, the register MOOS and you get a free ice cream or coffee

- DoubleTree Hotels: Complimentary warm chocolate chip cookie when you check in

- Zappos: Free upgrade of your shipping to next day

I'm proud to have my submission featured as Purple Goldfish Number 999, for Summit Bicycles in Burlingame, California. Here's my input:

I just visited Summit Bicycles in Burlingame and chatted with Chris who has been there many years now.

Chris is a good story all by himself. He started as a bicycle mechanic and learned the business from the ground up. Now he spends most of his time out on the floor helping customers. And he's great. Very knowledgeable about bikes and approachable.

I confirmed they still give that free tune-up with all new bikes. If this service is purchased separately, it would cost $90. And it's not just one tune-up a year. Bring your bike in as much as you like, there's no limit!

How do they justify all this free labor? It keeps customers coming back and provides some differentiation from Internet sellers competing only on price. Also, some tune-up customers end up buying parts if needed for repairs (the tune-up includes just service), or other accessories.

I bought my current bike a few years ago and it's still in good shape thanks to Summit's service. Every year in the spring I dust off the cobwebs and take it in for a tune-up. And usually end up buying a few other things, too.

Next time I'm in the market for a new bike, I'll buy it at Summit because they do more than just sell the bike. The free tune-up has both a real value ($90 x several years) to me and is good business for Summit, too.

Phelps identified twelve types of Purple Goldfish in two big categories of "value" and "maintenance." Use these examples to stimulate your own thinking and find creative ways to delight with a modest investment. Giving a little bit extra can pay huge dividends as customers spread positive word of mouth to their family, friends, and colleagues.

If the Customer Experience Is So Important, How Do You Explain the Success of Ryanair?

These days everyone seems to be talking about the customer experience. It's the key to competitive advantage, advocates say, because products are commodities and you can't compete on price unless you're Walmart.

Well, there's some truth to that. But I'd like to provide a reality check to the notion that a delightful or even good customer experience is always needed to drive profitable growth.

I've been hearing about Ryanair for the past few years—mostly horror stories about bad service and how the airline would never make it. Imagine my surprise when I read that Ryanair remains Europe's number-one customer service airline because, during January 2012:

- 91 percent of Ryanair's over thirty-three thousand flights arrived on time, up 1 percent on January 2011.

- Less than one complaint per thousand passengers was received.

- Less than one mislaid bag claim per two thousand passengers was received.

In that article, a Ryanair executive claimed that once passengers "have switched to Ryanair's prices these passengers keep coming back for our unbeatable on-time flights, fewest lost bags, and great customer service."[108]

Researching online, I found a lot of pros and cons about Ryanair. Some customers like the service (and love the ultra-low prices) others really hate the service and complain about rude employees, dirty cabins, and hidden fees.

I don't know how Ryanair can claim "great customer service" unless they define it as "we get you to your destination at a low price, and that's it." Nevertheless, Ryanair seems to be doing quite well financially. According to Ryanair's 2011 annual report, the airline is growing in passengers, revenue, and profits. Controversial CEO Michael O'Leary sums up: "Our 2011 net profit after tax of €401 million ($565 million) makes Ryanair the world's most profitable low-fares airline as highlighted by Air Transport World in July 2011."

Two other low-cost airlines—JetBlue and Southwest—were ranked second and ninth on this list. And these airlines are well known for providing good experiences. So what's the secret to Ryanair's success? Here's a sampling from CustomerThink community comments (minor edits for grammar and clarity):

- This is a perfect illustration of a business understanding what's important to the customer. Ryanair knows that its service can be left wanting in certain areas but in terms of what's important to the customer a bevy of smiling cabin attendants isn't high on the list.

- The reason that Ryanair continually "please" their customers is it has low customer expectations. Every time I board a Ryanair flight I don't care about the service or any lavish extras, that isn't the reason I booked. All I care about is the cheap price I have paid and arriving at my destination. Therefore, when I arrive at my destination and have more money to spend as a result of the cheap flight, I'm happy.

- Customer Experience is not all about sex appeal and customer service. It's about delivering on the promise of your brand. If Ryanair is all about low-cost travel that gets you there on time without losing your bags, then folks are buying into that.

- Ryanair doesn't have a complaint site on the net. To complain about their disrespectful and discriminating service you have to be at the airport during working hours.

- When you are not fully aware of all the "Ryanair-specific travel rules," you end up being charged more by Ryanair than by any regular airlines. Moreover, many newcomers simply lose completely their money and don't fly. And, they just feel stupid not to have read all the rules and done things in time!

- I compare Ryanair with trains, not with other carriers. Ryanair is cheaper, quicker, and better than trains, for the same distance. The only things I care about are price and security (I hope regulations and controls won't allow any carrier to compromise this).

One survey of over eight thousand travelers gave Ryanair a customer satisfaction rating of 38 percent (second worst), versus a less-than-stellar industry average of 51 percent. What's surprising is that the survey respondents gave Ryanair only "two stars out of five for value for money." I thought this was the main appeal of Ryanair.[109]

> Can you build a long-term strategy around unhappy customers that are loyal only to your price, until they can find another alternative?

My take is that Ryanair's price-only strategy works (for now) for two reasons. First, its low prices compete with nonairline forms of travel, such as trains and buses. Travelers on a limited budget will put up with bad service if it saves them hours of travel time. Second, Ryanair's low fares are deceptive—they don't represent the full price customers are likely to pay unless they can avoid the creative fees. Much like the banks inventing fees to boost earnings, the cost of the seat is just the beginning. Any misstep will generate a surprise charge.

The risk, however, is a low-cost airline offering Ryanair real competition on price and also friendly service. The customers that O'Leary says are loyal will defect immediately.

Time will tell whether Ryanair's strategy will work over the long term. The key question is: Can you build a long-term strategy around unhappy customers that are loyal only to your price, until they can find another alternative?

Three Roles for Technology in Customer Delight

Like it or not, the world is going digital. Websites were just the beginning. Now we have social media, mobile, and ever more exotic forms of automation like "Marie," a digital avatar that helps travelers in New York's La Guardia Airport.[110]

Since we haven't figured out how to create more hours in the day, the only conclusion I can reach is that more of our lives will be spent interacting with technology of one kind or another and less time interacting with human beings. Is that a bad thing? No, but as you'll learn, being "not bad" is not the same as being delightful.

The Digital Experience Conundrum

As a long-time Wells Fargo customer, I find the bank's ATMs well designed and efficient. Other banks provide a similar experience. One recent innovation is the ability to deposit checks without using envelopes. While I appreciate that new feature, I'm not likely to mention it when someone asks me about my banking experiences. Instead, I'd tell them the story I recounted earlier, when a banker gave great personal service to my mother.

In a 2006 customer experience study, I found that 70 percent of "memorable" experiences involved *people*. Why is that? Well, humans are more likely to be involved in complex customer situations—especially emotion-charged service incidents. In CustomerThink's research, we find that friendly, well-trained, and knowledgeable employees are key factors in customer experience excellence. Only humans can express empathy and solve problems creatively, so it's not surprising that interactions with people are more memorable.

Of course, people are also more inconsistent, as Larry Freed of ForeSee points out. You'll get more delightful experiences, but also more frustrating ones. Technology is less memorable, in part, because it doesn't have such variability, Freed contends.

The conundrum is that *digitizing more interactions may actually hurt company efforts to differentiate based on customer experience.* Why? Most companies use technology to make customer interactions more efficient, consistent, and *less memorable.* Sometimes technology can delight, but as Jon Picoult of

Watermark Consulting notes: "When technology helps fuel a delightful customer experience, it usually doesn't take much for other firms to copy that technology."

The solution to this conundrum is to understand the three important roles that technology can play in delightful customer experiences. Let's use the analogy of a great movie, where the audience experience is delivered by the star, supporting actors, and a "key grip" to manage lighting and camera movements. Obviously only the actors are seen on screen, but without great support behind the camera, a film won't be delightful to watch.

Technology as the Star of the Show

In some cases technology clearly is the lead actor. Take Amazon.com, which conducts its business exclusively online (good luck finding a phone number if you need help). The website doesn't try to wow customers on every visit. By stressing ease of use, personalized recommendations, and flawless delivery, it has earned stratospheric scores of eighty-six by the ACSI in 2011 and 76 percent in 2012 NPS benchmarks.

> Most companies use technology to make customer interactions more efficient, consistent, and *less memorable.*

Not surprisingly, Apple is another loyalty leader that excels in technology-based interactions (although its retail store experience shines, too). Bruce Temkin of Temkin Group says that voice-activated experiences, such as pioneered by Apple's Siri, will help create delight "if for no other reason than people aren't expecting them."

Asking Siri to find the nearest Chinese restaurant is amusing, but businesses also have a great opportunity to create voice-activated smartphone applications. USAA is planning such an application, a move consistent with the digital direction that Neff Hudson, assistant VP of emerging channels, revealed at a 2012 CXPA conference. He and other speakers acknowledged that one key challenge is maintaining empathetic and caring customer relationships in a world that is rapidly moving to digital interactions.

Design matters, too. For example, when booking flights, hotels, or car rentals, most travel sites function about the same. But Hipmunk innovates by providing flight options sorted by "agony"—a combination of price, duration, and number of stops. You also get a more intuitive visualization of the flight options, including layover times. For hotel search, you can see "heat maps" overlaid on a map to help decide where to stay based on restaurants, shopping, night life, etc. Other sites force you, as Forrester analyst Kerry Bodine puts it well, to do the "math in your head."

There's plenty of room for differentiation with creative use of current technology. And, for those who want to live on the bleeding edge, Bruce Kasanoff of Now Possible suggests looking at emerging technologies like Senseg, which turns touchscreens into "feel" screens, or Kinect-style gestural interfaces from Prime Sense.

Technology as Supporting Actor

Of course, not everyone can be the star. And even big stars sometimes serve as members of the supporting cast. Like Jack Nicholson, who won Oscars for his lead role in *One Flew Over the Cuckoo's Nest* and as best supporting actor in *Terms of Endearment*.

Technology, too, can play a supporting role "in front of the camera," adding value to the customer experience. Starbucks, for instance, has made its store experience a central part of its value proposition. Why else would someone pay four bucks for a frappuccino when you can make one for yourself for thirty-two cents?

Little conveniences can help a brand stand out in a "sea of sameness." Jeannie Walters of 360Connext believes that the mobile payment system Square helps create a "memorable experience where before there was nothing special, memorable, or intimate about it." Starbucks has announced a partnership with Square that will eventually enable customers to be recognized when they enter a store and pay by simply saying their names.[111]

Like pizza? Technology is ready to help! Domino's allows customers to track their pizzas online, and you can order pizzas and other food directly from iPhone apps. Traveling to Dubai? No problem. Pick up a VIP Pizza Magnet from the Red Tomato Pizza company for one-click ordering. Refrigerator not included.

Customers may have to engage more with brands to enable technology to do its thing. As Annette Franz Gleneicki of CX Journey notes, "In order for technology to come close to delighting, you have to train it or teach it what will delight you." For customers willing to convey their preferences, banks can send an email when a credit limit has been reached, airlines can rebook automatically, or call centers can call back instead of making customers wait on hold.

Technology as "Key Grip"

In filmmaking, a "key grip" is the person who manages lighting and camera movement. You don't see the key grip or the workers (grips), but if they didn't do their job well your movie experience would suffer.

Although rarely noticed, technology is often part of the infrastructure needed for employees to delight customers. Jeanne Bliss of CustomerBLISS says that "high-tech should enable high touch." From her prior experience at Lands' End, Bliss says technology enabled the retailer to automatically insert custom messages and "freebies" in shipping boxes when customers placed their first order, bought a certain category, etc.

Indeed, providing personalized and relevant recommendations is one crucial role in digital shopping sites like Amazon.com. I actually enjoy getting emails from Amazon.com promoting new books and other products because they are *relevant*—based on my purchasing history. Sampson Lee of G-CEM agrees: Using customer databases to tailor customized offers for VIP customers is a good example of technology-assisted delight. But it's the humans who often get credit for the delight, even when technology was required behind the scenes.

For retailers, having the right products is critical. According to Stan Phelps of 9 Inch Marketing, Izzy's Ice Cream Cafe of St. Paul (Minnesota, United States) serves over 150 flavors of handmade ice cream, but can only sell thirty-two flavors in the case at one time. By using RFID tags to identify each flavor when it is placed in the case ready to serve, customers can be notified by email within three minutes. (I've set my alert for Umeshu Chocolate, a dark chocolate ice cream made with Japanese plum wine. Yum.)

What's Your Action Plan for Digital Delight?

The foregoing provides a sampling of ideas and technologies to illustrate key roles for technology in customer delight. To maximize your success, here are recommended action steps:

- **Understand what drives delight versus dissatisfaction.** Technology can help minimize "dissatisfiers," drive "delighters," or both. It's critical to understand the difference. In banking, technology could contribute to delighting customers via a new mobile app, or by assisting bank personnel to consult more effectively with clients.

- **Decide what role technology should play.** Not every company can or should make technology the "star" in customer experiences. Visit the Zappos website and you'll find it nicely designed with snappy performance. However, you'll more likely be impressed by the 365-day return policy, free shipping, and amazing customer service if you need help with an order.

- **Keep innovating!** However you decide to use technology, it changes fast. As many experts noted, the "half-life" on digital innovations is short. Citibank was the first mover in mobile check deposits, but now all four of the largest US banks enable customers to deposit checks by scanning with smartphones. With good research and innovative thinking, you can use technology to directly or indirectly make a difference in customer experiences.

FOOD FOR THOUGHT

- Do you understand the difference between what dissatisfies versus delights your customers?
- What role will technology play in customer delight, either direct or indirect?
- Are your employees trained, empowered, and rewarded for delighting customers?
- Is cost a valid reason for lack of focus on delight? Or just an excuse?
- If technology is to be the "star," are you prepared to keep innovating?

Leadership

Between saying and doing, many a pair of shoes is worn out.
Italian proverb

My family has been a Sprint wireless customer for more than ten years. We're happy now, but six years ago we almost fired Sprint due to dropped calls, billing problems, and limited support for newer smartphones.

Ironically, if we had called to complain often enough, Sprint would have fired *us*!

That's right, in June 2007 Sprint fired about one thousand of its fifty-three million wireless customers for excessive calls to the contact center, mostly for billing and general account issues. In termination letters to offending customers, Sprint matter-of-factly said that "the number of inquiries you have made to us during this time has led us to determine that we are unable to meet your current wireless needs." Sprint generously zeroed out the affected customers' account balances and said it would not charge an early termination fee.[112]

Simple and straightforward. Imminently reasonable. What could possibly go wrong?

First, the decision set off a firestorm of mostly bad publicity at a time when the carrier was struggling to compete with other major wireless carriers (AT&T, T-Mobile, and Verizon). At the time, Sprint's customer satisfaction rating was 61, worst in the industry by a wide margin.[113]

Whoever said that "there's no such thing as bad publicity" is invited to explain how firing customers helped Sprint. I called company executives "Sprinting Idiots" in a comment on Graham Hill's 2007 CustomerThink blog post. Since then, that post has accumulated thousands of views—a fraction of the millions of negative impressions that the "Sprint 1000" incident precipitated.[114]

Second, and perhaps much more important, *Sprint didn't address the reasons for the excessive phone calls.* In a customer service equivalent of "shoot the messenger," management decided that since they had worked to resolve issues to "the best of our ability," the only option left was to cut loose customers it couldn't satisfy and cost too much to serve.

In the debate that raged on social media in the following months, some sided with Sprint's decision because it made economic sense. Why keep customers you can't serve at a profit? Many others pointed out that firing customers just deludes management that they have solved the underlying problems and doesn't factor in the cost of the negative publicity.

Worst to First: Sprint's Dramatic Turnaround

To deal with this big hot mess, Sprint's board of directors appointed Dan Hesse as the new CEO in December 2007. Shortly thereafter, Sprint posted a stunning $30 billion loss for 2007, much of it due to a write-down on the ill-conceived Nextel merger.

Hesse began his tenure by laying off four thousand employees and closing 125 stores. (No word on whether fired workers were invited to join the Sprint 1000 customers at another carrier.) In 2008 Sprint lost five million subscribers, resulting in a 32 percent year-to-year decline in wireless revenue. Dwindling cash reserves put the company at serious risk of going out of business.[115]

Fast forward five years and Hesse had accomplished an amazing turnaround. Sprint's ACSI score climbed ten points to an industry-leading seventy-one—the biggest improvement of any company in any industry—and was ranked number one in call center satisfaction. J.D. Power and Associates ranked Sprint best in the purchase experience among full-service wireless providers for the third year in a row. Revenue and subscriber growth returned, although financial performance was uneven, to put it mildly.[116]

How did Hesse do it? Given the bleak situation, he could have continued to slash costs, hunker down, and hope for a buyer to rescue the company. Instead, taking a customer-centric approach, he directed the organization to fix its customer service problems and innovate to increase value to customers.

Let's take a closer look at Sprint's turnaround though the lens of the five customer-centric habits.

Listen: Understand What Customers Value; Act on Their Feedback

In a July 2010 interview, Sprint's VP of customer experience, Jerry Adriano, spoke candidly about the company's problems and game plan. He told me their goal was to "improve the end-to-end customer life cycle experience so that customers would *choose* to stay with Sprint."

I emphasized "choose" because it's really the key to this entire turnaround. *Genuine loyalty is a choice by the customer, not a lock-in by the company.* Two-year contracts and employer-mandated phones can give the appearance of loyalty (retention) while unhappy customers are just waiting for the first chance to bolt.

Adriano says their research found the three biggest drivers of loyalty were:

- **Network quality:** Consumers have come to depend on their cell phones working reliably with good call quality.

- **Competitive pricing:** With most families having multiple subscribers, cost must be competitive to fit budgets.

- **Problem resolution:** While smartphones have expanded capabilities and created complexity, customers still expect problems to be resolved in a timely manner.[117]

Sprint "listened" to customer feedback using transactional data, customer escalations, industry benchmarks, and social media. Poor service experiences was determined to be the major culprit in customer dissatisfaction, which deteriorated due to cost cutting after the 2005 Nextel merger. In all, they identified thirty-five to forty problems driving dissatisfaction. One simple example was an "over engineered" rebate process that frustrated customers and drove unnecessary Sprint calls and store visits.

Think: Make Smart, Fact-Based Decisions

The current hype about "big data" and analytics might lead you to believe that you can feed data into an analytics tool and have the "answer" pop out. Nothing could be further from the truth.

In Sprint's case, Adriano's team needed to prioritize problems to be fixed, so they could drive stakeholders to address issues. Although he had CEO-level support, it didn't give his team a "sheriff's badge and a gun" to force change. Two initiatives helped motivate stakeholders:

- Documenting an "ideal customer experience" that detailed what customers expected and needed and identified areas for improvement

- Creating a compelling business case for fixing service problems based on cost per call, a well-established metric with clear business impact

Sprint had double the call volume of its competitors, which cost the company millions of dollars per year. This actually helped the business case, because fixing service issues was relatively easy to justify based on cutting call volume. Improving retention rates was an additional, albeit more long-term, benefit.

Certain problems required sophisticated cross-channel analytics to uncover. Lance Williams, Sprint's director of customer management, explained that in 2008 Sprint had the worst IVR customer satisfaction in the industry. Analytics revealed why customers quit an IVR interaction to call a live agent. Armed with this insight, they made usability improvements that vaulted Sprint's IVR customer satisfaction into an industry-leading position by Q4 2009. As a result, the contact center completed "tens of millions more calls" in the IVR in 2009 versus 2008. Sprint's customers were less frustrated and the carrier reaped huge cost savings.[118]

Empower: Give Employees Resources and Authority to Serve Customers

Unsurprisingly, given the dire straits of the company in 2008, employee feedback in Glassdoor noted major concerns about Sprint's future. Here's one review that illustrates a common perception:

> The company is lacking direction right now and with past troubles, the management is struggling to find a strategy to turn around the company. The recent layoffs have disrupted morale and efficiency in the company. News or rumors of future layoffs only make it difficult for employees to focus on their jobs. Constant reorgs are also to blame with efficiency as too many things changed too quickly, again without any direction.

No doubt low morale was a factor in poor customer experiences. In the commentary surrounding the Sprint 1000 debacle, many said that the excessive calls were the result of dealing with Sprint employees who could not take care of a problem, getting transferred around, and even being dropped and having to call back. In short, customers wanted more "one and done" calls.

I've written previously that authority, insights, and motivation are key to empowering call center agents to improve first call resolution (FCR) and delight customers. Sprint has invested in an array of call center technologies and software applications to help agents resolve service requests more effectively. However, it's not clear that any specific solution had a transformative impact. Rather, it was Hesse's decision to make customer experience a corporate goal, and the use of analytics to *focus on the right problems*, that made the biggest difference, in my view.

> Sprint's Social Media Ninjas program is a brilliant use of social media to unleash the influence of thousands of employees to rebuild its brand.

I do think Sprint made innovative use of social media to empower its employees to serve as "ambassadors" for the company. An offshoot of its "Employees Helping Customers" initiative, Social Media Ninjas was launched in 2010 to help improve Sprint's reputation using social media sites like Facebook, Twitter, and YouTube. Jennifer Sniderman, Sprint's group manager of employee communications, said the program was inspired by discussions about "how to leverage outreach to customers as a competitive advantage." Customers were taking to social media to vent about problems, so why not equip Sprint employees to engage and help? Sniderman said Ninjas were asked to "have an authentic conversation, talk about what you know, be friendly, help when you can, and answer questions."[119]

All too often, support issues are dumped on the contact center, including problems created in product development, marketing, or elsewhere. Sprint's Social Media Ninjas program is a brilliant use of social media to unleash the influence of thousands of employees to rebuild its brand. As of December 2012, 2,700 Ninjas were helping to improve Sprint's reputation using their personal networks to engage with customers. Inviting all employees to lend a hand helping customers also sends a message that delivering a great customer experience is everyone's responsibility.

By 2013 employee morale had noticeably improved. On Glassdoor, one account executive employed for eight years called his experience a "wild, awesome ride" and gives Sprint management good marks for innovation, cleaning out poor performers, and listening to employees. Hesse has earned a 79 percent approval rating, significantly better than his peers at major wireless carriers.

Create: Produce New Value for Customers and Company

Larger carriers AT&T and Verizon have low churn rates of approximately 1 percent per month for postpaid wireless, which means relatively few opportunities exist for Sprint to poach customers. Fast, reliable networks, the latest smartphones, and aggressive pricing are essential to woo new customers.

In 2008, while customer service improvements were under way, Hesse also got to work on better solutions and pricing. Shortly thereafter, Sprint launched unlimited data plans, one of the key reasons our family has remained loyal over the years. With service problems mostly in the past, good economics for the family reduces the motivation to switch.

Unfortunately for Sprint, AT&T got initial exclusive rights to Apple's iPhone when it was launched. In late 2011 Hesse finally added the iPhone, paying dearly for the privilege. He agreed to purchase 30.5 million units worth $20 billion, which will keep the company in the red for years.[120]

Still, I like the fact that Hesse went "all in" because without the latest phones, he has little chance to grow. Now that Samsung has become a strong number two in smartphones, Hesse will have more bargaining power in the future.

Sprint's network has also been a cause for concern. Over five years or so, Hesse wound down the Nextel network and transitioned customers to the main Sprint network. He is still behind his bigger rivals in rolling out the faster LTE networks, but hopes to catch up by the end of 2013.

Add it all up, and my take is that Sprint is still trailing on technology but makes up for it with more compelling all-you-can-eat contracts, which Hesse pledges to continue.

Delight: Exceed Expectations; Be Remarkable!

Sadly, "delight" is a word not often heard attributed to wireless telecom carriers. Much of Sprint's efforts to improve the customer experience I'd classify as fixing dissatisfiers that stimulate churn. At this point late in the book, I hope you remember that lack of pain is not the same as delight. To be a true industry leader and break out of commodity hell, delight is a critical strategy to differentiate and build genuine customer loyalty.

One huge challenge is that smartphone suppliers get credit for "wow" and carriers tend to get blamed for problems. A 2011 Harris Interactive study confirmed that more than two-thirds of US smartphone users surveyed experience network service issues during common activities like Internet searches, data downloads, watching videos, and social networking. Unfortunately nearly half the users blamed their wireless network provider for these issues.[121]

Sprint's overall customer satisfaction improved dramatically from a horrible fifty-six in 2008 to a competitive seventy-one in 2013, similar to its major rivals. However, smartphone vendors have enjoyed much higher ratings, especially Apple, which currently tops the charts at eighty-one, using ACSI's methodology.

Sprint and all wireless providers are in a difficult position, generally viewed as a utility. Forest Morgeson, director of research at ACSI, says wireless telecom is turning into a commoditized market, with similar services and pricing available from several suppliers. ACSI's research finds that smaller carriers (those grouped in ACSI's "all others" category) exceed expectations mainly by offering substantially better prices.

On that note, one of the bright spots for Sprint is the award-winning Boost Mobile, which offers no-contract phones and wireless service. Low pricing for unlimited usage, coupled with "shrinking payments" as a reward for loyalty, combine to make "value" a big drawing card.

So is price cutting the answer to delight? No, this is not a viable option for the big carriers, in my view. Customers already view wireless telecom as a utility; this would just be a race to the bottom that could only be won by the carrier with the lowest costs.

The answer may lie in understanding delighters by customer segment. Bain consultants Domenico Azzarello and Mark Kovac sum up the problem well: "With penetration flattening (wireless penetration in the United States, for example, is nearly 100 percent) and competition intensifying, companies must fight for market share as never before." Bain's research found that some customers like to be notified when they go over their plan limits, while others value a single point of contact, refunds for dropped calls, referral bonuses, etc.[122]

Leadership, Metrics, and Rewards

It should be obvious that Hesse's leadership is the main reason for Sprint's turnaround. While there is clearly more work needed, the company is in a much stronger position now. The recent merger with Softbank adds $5 billion of new capital to help fund the ongoing battle to deliver the best wireless experience.

It should also be clear that he didn't make this happen just with speeches and "the customer is king" proclamations. Here are key actions by Hesse that stand out to me:

1. Made the customer experience a top priority, then directed the organization to find and fix the problems that were causing customer dissatisfaction and churn

2. Focused on improving the core "product" being offered by upgrading the wireless network and (eventually) adding the iPhone and other leading smartphones

3. Recognized that price was a strong lever in a market increasingly viewed as a utility. Unlimited and lower-cost plans have helped Sprint battle back against much larger rivals AT&T and Verizon

To support these initiatives, Hesse also understood a key point about customer-centric "habits." Leaders must make new behaviors a part of the culture so it becomes the way business is done routinely. Tops on Hesse's "magnificent seven" change-drivers is "align compensation and rewards." Employees *must* be measured and rewarded for executing any business strategy.[123]

Looking back on their journey, Jerry Adriano said the three keys to Sprint's improvements are:

- **Fact based.** Analytics are critical to dissect customer experience problems because "it's hard to be successful just using opinion."

- **Long-term vision.** Must be able to define the "end state" that the organization is striving for and explain why the journey is worthwhile.

- **Collaboration.** Yes, strong leadership from the top is a must. But the importance of working with partners who will take suggestions and implement improvements "can't be overstated."

The role of chief service officer Bob Johnson (Adriano's boss) is also interesting. Pre-Hesse, Johnson helped the company execute a cost-cutting strategy. After Hesse changed direction, Johnson focused the organization on improving the customer experience. This suggests that the role of chief customer officers is still largely supportive of the company's business strategy, which must be driven by the CEO.

The Journey Continues

Sprint's turnaround from "worst to first" from 2008 through 2012 is remarkable. However, as this book goes to press, Sprint's position is competitive but hardly leading in all categories. Churn for postpaid contracts is still hovering around two percent per month, double its larger rivals. One reason: J.D. Power ranks Sprint well behind Verizon in network quality.[124]

This real-world example of five customer-centric habits at work shows there's not always a pot of gold at the end of the customer-centric rainbow. Sometimes customer-centricity keeps a company in the game to keep up the good fight so it can prevail another day. I hope Sprint does, because as a customer I like much of what the company is doing. And underdogs always make a good story!

Do You Need a Chief Customer Officer?

I used to think that the chief customer officer (CCO) would be a temporary job. I made this prediction in 2007 at a speaker's dinner before a conference keynote, then was embarrassed to find myself seated next to—you guessed it—a chief customer officer! Fortunately no food fight ensued, but we did have a spirited debate about why the job was needed and how long it would last.

My argument at that time was a CCO isn't needed if customer-centricity is a part of how a company does business. You rarely see such a job position at companies leading the pack in customer loyalty surveys. With CEO Jeff Bezos at the helm, Amazon.com doesn't need a chief customer officer. Cisco doesn't have one, either. At Zappos, it's clear that CEO Tony Hsieh is leading their customer-centric culture.

But since then, as I've done more research and developed my thinking about the five habits and customer-centric stages, I've found that the vast majority of companies could benefit from someone with this role. The reason why is simple: Precious few companies achieve Stage Four in their customer-centric maturity (as explained below), where a CCO is not needed because customer-centricity is engrained into the corporate culture.

For everyone else, the CCO is a leadership position that, in conjunction with the CEO, can help a company progress on its customer-centric journey.

Orchestrating Customer Experiences

According to a 2013 Forrest Research report, one of the key responsibilities of the CCO is "orchestrating" experiences.[125] I agree and like this term a lot. It's been clear to me for a few years that poorly coordinated multi-channel interactions are a huge source of customer frustration. In 2010 I wrote about the need to "harmonize" the cross-channel experience, and I've used the analogy of an orchestra conductor in speeches since then. That "conductor" can be the CCO.

"Chief customer officer" remains the most popular term for the "executive leading customer experience (CX) efforts across a business unit or an entire company." Forrester says they've found 730 such leaders, and 45 percent have the CCO title while chief experience officer came in second at just 18 percent.

I was pleased to learn that 85 percent of CCOs sit on the executive management team, a big jump from just 50 percent in 2012. Thankfully, it seems that few companies give the CCO title to a lower level staff position—like someone responsible for rolling up customer satisfaction reports for the company. That's important, but not really a leadership role with enough clout. CCOs are most likely to come from prior jobs in operations/process/quality, line-of-business management, or marketing. Less commonly, from sales and customer service.

Jeanne Bliss, a former CCO and author of *Chief Customer Officer: Getting Past Lip Service to Passionate Action,* says the "optimum organization" is a staff organization with a dedicated team, reporting "as high up inside the organization as required, based on the level of change needed."[126] Even if not reporting directly to the CEO (which I would personally recommend), the CCO should clearly be empowered by the CEO.

A Forrester research report says one precondition for success is a "strategic mandate," which means "the executive team must define the purpose for appointing a CCO, build customer experience into the company strategy, and adopt companywide customer experience metrics that correlate with key business performance outcomes."

Should Silos Be Busted or Tamed?

If you had a serious health problem, who would you want to diagnose and treat your condition? A specialist, of course. Organization silos such as marketing, sales, support, and product development will never go away because companies need specialists to get jobs done right.

But when customers have to interact with multiple departments, it can be very frustrating. The problem is that as organizations grow and become more specialized and complicated, they tend to have more silos on the inside while offering more customer interaction channels on the outside. The combination can be deadly, because there are lots of opportunities for things to go wrong. Customers won't get a loyalty-building experience and the company, as vividly illustrated in the Sprint turnaround story, can waste massive amounts of resources fixing these cross-channel or cross-silo problems.

While specialization is needed, so is coordination and cooperation. Bliss says the CCO position is well suited for large, complex organizations that need help with a mission to "pull our organization together and unite efforts to deliver a deliberate customer experience." That's what Bliss aptly calls a "human duct tape role" to improve coordination between silos. Metrics are at the source of the problem, because each silo tends to get rewarded for performing its specialty well, even when "success" in one silo causes problems in another.[127]

I believe one answer is to make sure that silos that should be collaborating have shared goals and metrics. You're not going to get rid of silos. "Busting silos" is not the mission of the CCO, it should be helping collaborate and serve customers better. This collaboration should start, says Bliss, with annual planning processes, where leaders "start in a united way" to define priorities, responsibilities, and funding.

Customer-centric Maturity Stages

As discussed earlier, customer-centricity has been cast by various industry experts as targeting customers, selling more products to the same customers, or doing whatever customers ask. Still, most people have some vague idea that being customer-centric means building loyal relationships.

In my view, customer-centricity is not a black-and-white proposition. Most companies can claim to be customer-centric to one degree or another. I see customer-centricity as a journey, not a destination. To progress, companies generally evolve through four stages of development under the leadership of the CEO.

1. **Targeted *on* Customers:** to sell more products and services to the "best" customers

2. **Responsive *to* Customers:** to make improvements by acting on customer feedback

3. **Engaged *with* Customers:** creating an emotional bond that drives advocacy behavior

4. **Inspired *by* Customers:** developing new solutions to solve problems before customers ask!

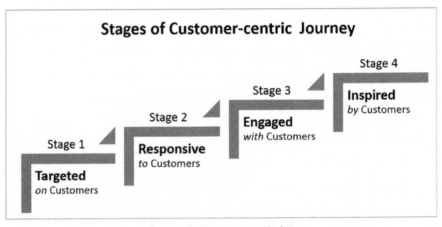

© Copyright 2014 CustomerThink Corp.

Now this might suggest that companies start at Stage 1 and progress to Stage 4 over time. Some do, but that's not the only pattern. Think about new companies that bring innovative solutions to the market to rave reviews by their customers. But later, as the business grows, they can't duplicate that initial hit and lose touch with their customers. Calcification sets in, and the firm devolves to aggressive marketing and selling to push solutions without dealing with customer problems. Eventually, the company will disappear or be acquired.

Also, while it's true that most stage-four companies are highly profitable, it doesn't mean you can't make money at other stages. For example, large US retail banks don't earn high loyalty ratings. The ACSI average for the banking industry was a respectable seventy-seven in 2012. However, *all* of the major US banks (JPMorgan Chase, Wells Fargo, Citigroup, and Bank of America) were below average. The "other" firms—mostly regional banks and credit unions—averaged seventy-nine to bring up the industry average.

According to 2013 research by PeopleMetrics, community banks do a much better job creating an emotional bond in relationships where customers feel "valued," "appreciated," and "cared for." National banks are focusing more on digital interactions (e.g., mobile banking) and internal automation.[128]

But banks and other stage-one companies can continue to profit so long as their major competitors do the same. They leverage technology, improve their targeting, closing techniques, and so on to maximize their return. This is the CRM or "value extraction" thinking that dominates the corporate world.

This opens the door for generally smaller and more innovative firms to focus on increasing value *delivery*. The innovators in retail banking are small firms like Ally and Umpqua in the US, and First Direct and Metro in the UK. These firms try harder to delight their customers and deliver innovative solutions. Eventually, if enough customers shift to the upstarts, these firms will become the new leaders in retail banking.

Let's take a closer look at the four stages.

Stage 1: Targeted on Customers

Mantra: "We know our customers and what they buy and optimize marketing, sales, and customer service activities to generate more revenue and profit for the company."

This is where most CRM efforts start and end. It's not really about the customer; it's about the customer's money! A classic example of this is Ryanair, which by all accounts has been successful with a low-cost strategy aimed at a price-sensitive segment of the European air travel market. Passengers have little good to say about their experience, leading many to question whether the model is sustainable when more customer-friendly competitors emerge. Still, the model is working; low price can drive retention-based loyalty for some customers.

There are many examples of process automation delivering a solid ROI, including CRM projects that deliver a good payback two-thirds of the time. However, benefits tend to be more tactical: streamlined processes, improved decision-making, and lower cost. Improving customer loyalty, a key selling point in CRM's heyday, has not been reported as an outcome in the majority of CRM projects.

Stage 2: Responsive to Customers

Mantra: "We regularly get customer feedback, prioritize key issues, and work to improve customer satisfaction with the products and services we sell, to minimize customer attrition."

In the past few years we've seen a rush to gather feedback and fix customer problems, with Voice of Customer initiatives using Enterprise Feedback Management (EFM) technology. In part to differentiate, but let's be honest, the growing power of "social customers" has made customer satisfaction mission-critical. Just ask United Airlines, which suffered as a result of the United Breaks Guitars incident. A video uploaded

July 6, 2009, by the aggrieved musician Dave Carroll had accumulated thirteen million views in the following four years.[129]

Unfortunately, most companies are stuck in "fix it" mode and haven't figured out yet how to create innovative experiences that delight customers. A few years ago, Sprint struggled with quality of service (e.g., dropped calls) and customer support issues that caused customers to churn. They eventually fixed both to return to a competitive position. However, industry leadership usually requires more than "not screwing up."

Stage 3: Engaged with Customers

Mantra: "We focus on a long-term relationship and strive to make an emotional connection with customers by providing delightful experiences that create advocates."

When I think of long-term relationships, my mind wanders back to my days at IBM. While products were not always great, customers trusted IBM to stick with them over the long term, and there was a two-way dialog especially with larger accounts. Cisco has a similar mind-set. In a discussion with an executive there, I learned they regularly assess what drives customer loyalty and make frequent adjustments.

For B2C, Zappos is the quintessential example because founder/CEO Tony Hsieh has made amazing customer service a differentiator and integral to their culture. Once I bet someone $100 that if they contacted Zappos about a problem, they would be happy with how it was handled. I didn't lose my bet!

Stage 4: Inspired by Customers

Mantra: "We think deeply about what customers are trying to accomplish in their business and personal lives and create new ways to add value before they ask!"

In my research, I found that less than 10 percent of companies reach this stage. Those that do earn outsized returns. Of course Apple is the quintessential example. Despite the folklore that Steve Jobs didn't do customer research, Apple worked very hard to understand what customers needed and desired, then innovated to produce a string of hits starting with the iPod more than a decade ago. Meanwhile, Nokia, Blackberry, Sony, and other former handset leaders missed opportunities to integrate consumer electronics and mobile devices.

Another great example is Homeplus—Tesco's attempt to enter the South Korean grocery market. Tesco researchers found that busy South Korean workers viewed shopping as a chore to be done at the end of a long day. In other words, they just wanted the goods, not the in-store shopping experience. So Tesco created a virtual store in subway stations where consumers could view and order groceries to be delivered straight to their home.

Where Are You in Your Journey?

The vast majority (roughly 70 percent) of companies are at the first two stages of their customer-centric journey. Most companies try to focus their marketing/sales/service activities *on* customers to extract the greatest value.

A smaller but growing number of companies also ask for feedback so they can improve products and fix customer service issues. But despite all the rhetoric about customer experience, delighting customers and innovating, it's quite rare in practice.

Now, you may not agree with my labels, and that's perfectly fine. Create your own labels! What's important is the progression from an organization that targets customers to extract value from a customer base to a fully customer-centric firm that excels at *delivering* value based on a deep understanding of customers' needs, wants, and desires.

Wherever you are on your customer-centric journey, keep moving. And good luck!

Afterword

Why are some companies so obviously customer-centric, trying very hard to please their customers at every turn, while others, frankly, don't seem to give a damn? Customer-centricity is an elusive concept, difficult to define and even more difficult for some companies to comprehend and deliver. But customers know and appreciate it when they see it, and they reward customer-centric firms with their loyalty.

In *Hooked on Customers*, Bob Thompson makes a compelling case for what it takes to become a customer-centric organization and the rewards that are likely to flow to firms that achieve this position. Drawing on his considerable experience with some of the world's leading companies, he has prepared an essential guide for business leaders who wish to take their firms down the road to customer-centricity.

Thompson makes it clear that, for some legendary firms, their focus on the customer comes naturally; it's in their culture and in their genes. But how did they get that way? What is it that distinguishes them from others who treat customers with much less care and respect?

The insight that he has gleaned from the many examples quoted in this book provides us with a valuable look inside those firms that may honestly be labeled customer-centric and that are, more importantly, acknowledged by their customers to be so. For those firms to which customer-centricity does not come quite so naturally, this book is a valuable guide to organizational change.

Through exhaustive research and study of leading firms, Thompson has identified the five essential abilities of leading customer-centric companies. He encourages leaders to *listen*, to commit the necessary resources to obtain the insight needed to truly understand customers; to *think*, to devote deep thought to identifying the implications of data; to *empower*, giving employees the freedom they need to please and impress customers; to *create*, constantly looking for new ways to create value for customers; and to *delight*, moving beyond mere customer satisfaction to deliver a combination of surprise and emotional value.

Further, he observes that the most effective firms have succeeded in *institutionalizing* customer-centricity, in making it part of the culture of the firm and of how all employees conduct themselves. Customer-centricity is not a loyalty program; it is not CRM or CEM; it is not social media. It is an attitude that humanizes customers and places them at the center of organizational decision-making, an attitude that is shared by all employees. To make this happen requires leadership from the top and a commitment to the customer that reinforces that attitude at every turn.

This book is essential reading for CEOs, CMOs, CCOs, and other executives whose goal is to differentiate their firms through a genuine commitment to customers. Customer-centricity that is more than lip service must start at the top; it can't be driven from the middle ranks of an organization.

Bob Thompson's new book won't help those firms whose leaders are reluctant to make that commitment or do not understand what it means to be truly customer-centric. If your firm really believes in the potential to be achieved through a real focus on and commitment to your customers, use this book as your guide to building solid, lasting, genuine, and profitable customer relationships.

Jim Barnes
Chief customer strategist at BMAI, author of *Build Your Customer Strategy*
St. John's, Newfoundland, Canada

Acknowledgments

I've been blessed to know and collaborate with many of the world's thought leaders in customer-centric business, largely facilitated by the CustomerThink online community. Each of CustomerThink's fifteen hundred authors has contributed in some way to this book. However, a few industry colleagues and authors deserve special thanks for their steadfast support of our community and influence on the concepts I've presented in this book.

I'll begin with a special thanks to Jim Dickie and Barry Trailer, B2B sales thought leaders who inspired me to join the CRM industry and launch my firm in 1998. I also owe a great debt to Bill Brendler, Mei Lin Fung, and Dick Lee, three brave souls who joined me to volunteer time to answer questions as the first "CRM.Talk Gurus." That was the start of our development as a real online community.

To cover the many facets of a customer-centric business, our community has grown enormously over the years. My heartfelt thanks to the following experts for enriching my life and supporting our community:

- Customer-centric leadership: Jim Barnes, Jeanne Bliss, Tony Craddock, Maz Iqbal, Doug Leather, and David Rance

- CRM: William Band, Silvana Buljan, Francis Buttle, Jay Curry, Jack Fujieda, Paul Greenberg, Graham Hill, Rafael Rodriquez, Ed Thompson, Brian Vellmure, and Wil Wurtz

- CEM: Michael Hinshaw, Lynn Hunsaker, Sampson Lee, Stan Phelps, Colin Shaw, Shaun Smith, and Bruce Temkin

- Analytics: Gary Cokins, Jill Dyché, Seth Grimes, Laura Patterson, Eric Siegel, and Jim Sterne

- Innovation: Robert Brands, Bruce Kasanoff, Stefan Lindegaard, Patricia Seybold, and Tony Ulwick

- Digital marketing: Ardath Albee, Akin Arikan, Naras Eechambadi, Dan McDade, Jon Miller, David Raab, Alan See, Steve Woods, and Tony Zambito

- B2B sales: Bob Apollo, Dave Brock, Donal Daly, Jack Dean, Jim Dickie, John Holland, Andy Rudin, and Barry Trailer

- Customer service: Chip Bell, Shep Hyken, Kate Leggett, and Bill Price

- Customer loyalty: Jill Griffin, Bob Hayes, Howard Lax, and Michael Lowenstein

- Outside-in process: Mike Boysen, Joseph Dager, and Dick Lee

- Social business: Vanessa DiMauro, Jacob Morgan, Axel Schultze, and Guy Stephens

- Contact center: Peggy Carlaw, Donna Fluss, and Jodie Monger

I also want to express my sincere appreciation for the outstanding work of CustomerThink staff. Our first website was launched by Matt Carroll, who handled all web publishing and discussion moderation in those exciting early days. Carol Smalley and Gwynne Young both made huge editorial contributions at different stages of our development. David Sims wrote about CRM industry developments with style and humor. Jennie Greer has been the mainstay of our support operation for more than ten years, epitomizing great customer service.

Notes

Much of the information presented in this book came from the author's in-person, phone and email interviews with representatives of the companies described. Facts and quotes that do not have a note are from these personal interviews. The notes include cited web addresses available at the time the book was written.

Introduction

[1] "Leading Through Connections: Insights from the IBM Global CEO Study," IBM (paper), 2012, http://www-935.ibm.com/services/us/en/c-suite/ceostudy2012/.

[2] "History of Southwest Airlines," AvStop.com (article), accessed July 2013, http://avstop.com/history/historyofairlines/southwest.html.

[3] "ACSI Methodology," The ACSI, accessed July 2013, http://www.theacsi.org/about-acsi/acsi-methodology.

[4] "CFI Group: Research Links Customer Satisfaction to Stock Returns," CFI Group (press release), July 5, 2012, http://cfigroup.com/downloads/Customer_Satisfaction_and_Stock_Returns_CFI_Group.pdf.

[5] Robert J. Allio, "Russell L. Ackoff, Iconoclastic Management Authority, Advocates a 'Systemic' Approach to Innovation," University of Pennsylvania (Ackoff Collaboratory for Advancement of the Systems Approach), 2003, http://www.acasa.upenn.edu/p19.pdf.

[6] Bob Thompson, "Revenue Performance Management (RPM): Strategy, Technology or the Real CRM 2.0?", CustomerThink (article), June 2, 2012, http://www.customerthink.com/article/revenue_performance_management_strategy_technology_real_crm_2_0.

A Brief History

[7] Bob Thompson, "Successful CRM: Turning Customer Loyalty into Profitability, CustomerThink (white paper), October 2004.

[8] "From Social Media to Social CRM," IBM (white paper), February 2011, http://public.dhe.ibm.com/common/ssi/ecm/en/gbe03391usen/GBE03391USEN.PDF.

[9] Jeremiah Owyang, "Social CRM: The New Rules of Relationship Management," March 5, 2010, Slideshare, http://www.slideshare.net/jeremiah_owyang/social-crm-the-new-rules-of-relationship-management.

[10] Sampson Lee, "Customer-Centricity Is Not the Solution; It's the Problem," CustomerThink (blog), July 20, 2012, http://www.customerthink.com/blog/customer_centricity_is_not_the_solution_it_s_the_problem.

[11] Don Peppers, "Explaining Customer Centricity with a Diagram," LinkedIn (blog), July 23, 2013, http://www.linkedin.com/today/post/article/20130123164215-17102372-explaining-customer-centricity-with-a-diagram.

[12] "TERM (Technology-Enabled Relationship Management)," Gartner, accessed July 2013, http://www.gartner.com/it-glossary/term-technology-enabled-relationship-management/.

[13] Bob Thompson, "The Next Generation of Customer Management? Customer Experience Management," CustomerThink (article), June 26, 2006, http://www.customerthink.com/article/cem_next_generation_crm.

[14] John Radcliffe, "Eight Building Blocks of CRM: A Framework for Success," Gartner, December 13, 2001, http://www.gartner.com/2_events/crmawards/2006/docs/buildingblocks.pdf.

[15] Bob Thompson interview with Ed Thompson of Gartner, "What's New with CRM, Social CRM and CEM?", CustomerThink (interview), February 24, 2012, http://www.customerthink.com/interview/whats_new_crm_social_crm_cem_inside_scoop_ed_thompson.

[16] Paul Hagen, "Beyond CRM: Manage Customer Experiences," Forrester Research (report), April 29, 2011, http://www.forrester.com/Beyond+CRM+Manage+Customer+Experiences/fulltext/-/E-RES57933?objectid=RES57933.

[17] Bruce Temkin, "The Ascendance of Customer-Centric Culture," 1to1media.com (blog), February 3, 2011, http://www.1to1media.com/weblog/2011/02/guest_blogger_bruce_temkin_the.html.

[18] Maz Iqbal, "The Customer Loyalty Paradox (Part II): What We Can Learn from Richard Shapiro and the Welcomer Edge," CustomerThink (blog comment), March 6, 2012, http://www.customerthink.com/blog/the_customer_loyalty_paradox_part_ii.

Habit 1—Listen

[19] Ben Popken, "Walmart Declutters Aisles Per Customers' Request, Then Loses $1.85 Billion In Sales," Consumerist (article), April 18, 2011, http://consumerist.com/2011/04/18/walmart-declutters-aisles-per-customer-request-then-loses-185-billion-in-sales/.

[20] Interview with Chris Travell, Maritz Research, May 2, 2012.

[21] Interview with David VanAmburg, The ACSI, August 27, 2013.

[22] Interview with Howard Lax, GfK Customer Loyalty, April 11, 2012.

[23] "Customer Loyalty in Retail Banking: North America 2010," Bain (report), October 6, 2010, http://www.bain.com/Images/Customer_loyalty_in_retail_banking.pdf.

[24] "The 2011 Walker Loyalty Report for Information Technology," Walker (report), 2011.

[25] Interview with Karen Mangia, Cisco, April 24, 2012.

[26] Gina Sverdlov, "Brand Engagement the Consumer Way," Forrester (report), September 18, 2012, http://www.forrester.com/Brand+Engagement+The+Consumer+Way/fulltext/-/E-RES82301.

[27] "The Net Promoter Debate: An Interview with Tim Keiningham, Senior Vice President, Ipsos Loyalty," Admap, May 2007.

[28] Larry Freed, "Rethinking Net Promoter®: Serious Flaws Tarnish Simple Idea," ForeSee Results (paper), October 2007.

[29] Bob Thompson, "Use Text Analytics to Listen to Customers on Their Terms," CustomerThink (blog), August 31, 2007, http://www.customerthink.com/blog/text_analytics_listen_to_customers.

[30] Interviews conducted in September 2007 with managers at Egg, FileNet, and Thermo Fisher Scientific.

[31] James Borg, *Body Language: 7 Easy Lessons to Master the Silent Language*, FT Press, 2010.

[32] Adam Ostrow, "Inside Gatorade's Social Media Command Center," Mashable (article), June 15, 2010, http://mashable.com/2010/06/15/gatorade-social-media-mission-control.

[33] Bob Thompson, "Blind Spots in Your Online Customer Experience," CustomerThink (blog), September 19, 2008, http://www.customerthink.com/blog/online_customer_experience_blind_spots.

[34] Donna Fluss, "Customer Retention Is a Priority for Mobile Phone Providers," CustomerThink (article), January 15, 2009, http://www.customerthink.com/article/customer_retention_priority_mobile_phone_providers.

[35] Scott A. Neslin, Sunil Gupta, Wagner Kamakura, Junxiang Lu, and Charlotte H. Mason, "Defection Detection: Measuring and Understanding the Predictive Accuracy of Customer Churn Models," *Journal of Marketing Research*, May 2006.

[36] Bob Thompson, "Use Text Analytics to Listen to Customers on Their Terms," CustomerThink (blog), August 31, 2007, http://www.customerthink.com/blog/text_analytics_listen_to_customers.

[37] Bob Thompson, "Use Speech Analytics to Reduce Calls That Frustrate Customers and Hurt Productivity," CustomerThink (article), November 20, 2008, http://www.customerthink.com/article/speech_analytics_contact_center_experience.

[38] Bob Thompson, "Caesars Palace #Fails in 'Horrible' Checkout Experience," CustomerThink (blog), November 13, 2010,

http://www.customerthink.com/blog/caesers_palace_fails_in_horrible_checkout_experience.

[39] Bob Thompson interview with Jerry Adriano of Sprint, "Sprint Answers the Call to Improve Customer Experience," CustomerThink (interview), July 22, 2010, http://www.customerthink.com/interview/jerry_adriano_sprint_customer_experience.

[40] Daniel Thomas, "Tripadvisor Influences £500m Of Corporate Hotel Choices," Caterer and Hotel Keeper (article), http://www.caterersearch.com/Articles/09/10/2009/330333/TripAdvisor-influences-163500m-of-corporate-hotel.htm.

[41] Milan Patel, "How User-Generated Review Websites Impact a Hotel's RevPar," University of Nevada, Las Vegas (paper), April 1, 2011.

[42] "Best Western Cares," Hotel Interactive, June 28, 2010, http://www.hotelinteractive.com/article.aspx?articleid=17431.

[43] "Hotel Benchmarks by Company," The ACSI, accessed July 2013, http://www.theacsi.org/?option=com_content&view=article&id=147&catid=14&Itemid=212&i=Hotels.

Habit 2—Think

[44] "A Culture of Think," IBM, accessed July 2013, http://www-03.ibm.com/ibm/history/ibm100/us/en/icons/think_culture/.

[45] David Berreby, "Emonomics," *The New York Times*, March 16, 2008, http://www.nytimes.com/2008/03/16/books/review/Berreby-t.html.

[46] David T. Neal and Wendy Wood, "Automaticity in Situ: The Nature of Habit in Daily Life," Duke University, March 2007.

[47] James Temple, "U.S. Internet speed better but still lags," *San Francisco Chronicle*, January 26, 2013.

[48] Traffic and Market Data Report, Ericsson, November 2011, http://hugin.info/1061/R/1561267/483187.pdf.

[49] Jon Picoult, "The Watermark Consulting 2013 Customer Experience ROI Study," WaterRemarks (blog), April 2, 2013, http://www.watermarkconsult.net/blog/2013/04/02/the-watermark-consulting-2013-customer-experience-roi-study/.

[50] "Big data: The next frontier for competition," McKinsey.com, accessed July 2013, http://www.mckinsey.com/features/big_data.

[51] Keri Pearlson, "Analytics versus Intuition," International Institute for Analytics, January 21, 2011, http://iianalytics.com/2011/01/analytics-versus-intuition/.

[52] Bob Thompson interview with Karl Rexer, "Big Data and Analytics in a Customer-Focused Enterprise," CustomerThink (interview), August 7, 2012, http://www.customerthink.com/interview/big_data_analytics_customer_focused_enterprise_inside_scoop_with_karl_rexer.

[53] Bob Thompson, "8 Big Ideas for #CX Success (Highlights from Customer Experience Summit 2011)," CustomerThink (blog), November 10, 2011, http://www.customerthink.com/blog/customer_experience_summit_2011_8_big_ideas.

[54] "Wireless Telephone Service Benchmarks," The ACSI, accessed July 2013, http://www.theacsi.org/index.php?option=com_content&view=article&id=147&catid=14&Itemid=212&i=Wireless+Telephone+Service.

Habit 3—Empower

[55] Kara Swisher, "Physically Together": Here's the Internal Yahoo No-Work-From-Home Memo for Remote Workers and Maybe More," All Things D, February 22, 2013, http://allthingsd.com/20130222/physically-together-heres-the-internal-yahoo-no-work-from-home-memo-which-extends-beyond-remote-workers/.

[56] "Google," Glassdoor, accessed July 2013, http://www.glassdoor.com/Overview/Working-at-Google-EI_IE9079.11,17.htm.

[57] "Employee Engagement: What's Your Engagement Ratio?", Gallup, 2008, http://www.gallup.com/file/strategicconsulting/121535/Employee_Engagement_Overview_Brochure.pdf.

[58] James K. Harter, Frank L. Schmidt, Sangeeta Agrawal, Stephanie K. Plowman, "The Relationship Between Engagement at Work and Organizational Outcomes," Gallup, February 2013, http://www.gallup.com/strategicconsulting/126806/Q12-Meta-Analysis.aspx.

[59] Benjamin Schneider, Paul J. Hanges, D. Brent Smith, and Amy Nicole Salvaggio, "Which Comes First: Employee Attitudes or Organizational Financial and Market Performance?", *Journal of Applied Psychology*, February 10, 2003.

[60] James K. Harter, Frank L. Schmidt, James W. Asplund, Emily A. Killham, and Sangeeta Agrawal, "Causal Impact of Employee Work Perceptions on the Bottom Line of Organizations," *Perspectives on Psychological Science*, July 2010.

[61] Karl Moore, "Employees First, Customers Second: Why It Really Works in the Market," *Forbes* (blog), May 14, 2012, http://www.forbes.com/sites/karlmoore/2012/05/14/employees-first-customers-second-why-it-really-works-in-the-market/.

[62] https://www.jottit.com/v5wux/

[63] Michael Lowenstein, "Employee Ambassadorship and Advocacy: Living the Promise of 'Wow' Customer Value Delivery (Part I)," CustomerThink (blog), May 5, 2012, http://www.customerthink.com/blog/employee_ambassadorship_and_advocacy_living_the_promise_of_wow_customer_value_delivery_part_i.

[64] Richard A. Lee and David J. Mangen, "Customers Say What Companies Don't Want to Hear," HYM Press, 2006, http://www.customerthink.com/report/customers_say_what_companies_dont_want_hear.

[65] Robert Reiss, "How Ritz-Carlton Stays at the Top," *Forbes* (blog), October 30, 2009, http://www.forbes.com/2009/10/30/simon-cooper-ritz-leadership-ceonetwork-hotels.html.

[66] Omer Minkara, "Agent Desktop Optimization: Agents Can Finally Focus on the Customer," Aberdeen Group, October 1, 2012.

[67] "Agent Rewards and Recognition Report," *Call Center Management Review*, 2006.

[68] "First-Contact Resolution," ICMI Press (report), 2008.

[69] "Does Your Contact Center Measure First-Call Resolution?", ICMI (quick poll), initially posted May 9, 2011, http://www.icmi.com/Resources/Polls/Does-your-contact-center-measure-first-call-resolution.

[70] Bill Price, "Contact Center Metrics: AHT Is Out, FCR Is In (But Not Enough!)," CustomerThink (article), February 26, 2013, http://www.customerthink.com/article/contact_center_metrics_aht_is_out_fcr_is_in.

[71] Bob Thompson interview with Tammy Weinbaum of American Express, "Empower Your People to Drive Customer Experience ROI," CustomerThink (interview), January 5, 2012, http://www.customerthink.com/interview/tammy_weinbaum_american_express_empower_your_people_to_drive_customer_experience_roi.

[72] Greg Levin, "Zappos Customer Loyalty Team," Off Center (blog), January 3, 2011, http://www.offcenterinsight.com/2/category/zappos%20 customer%20loyalty%20team/1.html.

[73] Richard Foster, "Creative Destruction Whips through Corporate America," *Innosight* (Executive Summary), Winter 2012.

[74] "Business and Web 2.0: An interactive feature," McKinsey.com, March 2013, http://www.mckinsey.com/insights/business_technology/ business_and_web_20_an_interactive_feature.

[75] Dennis Howlett, "Enterprise 2.0: What a Crock," ZDNet, August 26, 2009, http://www.zdnet.com/blog/howlett/enterprise-2-0-what-a-crock/1228.

[76] Bob Thompson, "2011: The Year When 80% of Social CRM Projects Will #Fail…," CustomerThink (blog), January 4, 2011, http://www. customerthink.com/blog/2011_the_year_when_80_percent_of_social_ crm_projects_will_fail.

[77] Connie Chan and Jacob Morgan, "State of Enterprise 2.0 Collaboration," Chess Media Group (report), Q2/2011, http://www.chessmediagroup. com/resource/state-of-enterprise-2-0-collaboration/.

[78] Charlene Li, "Report: Making the Business Case for Enterprise Social Networks," Altimeter Group (blog), February 22, 2012, http://www. altimetergroup.com/2012/02/making-the-business-case-for-enterprise- social-networks.html.

79 Data supplied by Moxie Software, from Harris Interactive survey conducted February 27–29, 2012.

80 Gary Kelly, "A Message from Our CEO—Open Season on Assigned Seating," Nuts About Southwest (blog), June 21, 2006, http://www.blogsouthwest.com/blog/a-message-from-our-ceo-open-season-on-assigned-seating.

81 Jennifer Reingold, "Southwest's Herb Kelleher: Still crazy after all these years," *CNNMoney*, January 14, 2013, http://management.fortune.cnn.com/2013/01/14/kelleher-southwest-airlines/.

82 Katie J.M. Baker, "Cover Your Cleavage for Takeoff: Southwest Airlines Screws Up Again," Jezebel, June 4, 2012, http://jezebel.com/5917845/cover-your-cleavage-for-takeoff-southwest-airlines-screws-up-again.

83 Tamara Cohen, "Ryanair Puts Up Luggage Charges In Time for Summer (And Passengers Will Have to Pay to Use the Toilet Too)," MailOnline, April 7, 2010, http://www.dailymail.co.uk/news/article-1264006/Ryanair-hikes-luggage-charges-summer-toilet-tax-phased-in.html.

Habit 4—Create

84 "'You've Got to Find What You Love,' Jobs Says," *Stanford Report*, June 14, 2005, http://news.stanford.edu/news/2005/june15/jobs-061505.html.

85 "Jeff Bezos on Leading for the Long Term at Amazon," HBR Ideacast, January 3, 2013, http://blogs.hbr.org/ideacast/2013/01/jeff-bezos-on-leading-for-the.html.

[86] "What Is SD Logic?", *Service-Dominant Logic*, accessed July 2013, http://www.sdlogic.net/.

[87] "Ideation," Emerging Media, accessed July 2013, http://www.emerging mediaresearchcouncil.com/wp-content/uploads/2011/02/EMRC-Ideation.pdf.

[88] Bob Thompson interview with Tony Ulwick of Strategyn, "Customer-Centric Innovation Is Driven by Outcomes, Not Ideas," February 7, 2013, http://www.customerthink.com/interview/customer_centric_innovation_is_driven_by_outcomes_not_ideas.

[89] Yahoo Finance, accessed July 2013, http://finance.yahoo.com/echarts.

[90] Bob Thompson, "The ONE Thing You Need to Know About Net Promoter…," CustomerThink (blog), February 9, 2011, http://www.customerthink.com/blog/the_one_thing_you_need_to_know_about_net_promoter.

[91] "Transcript: Laura Lang, John Riccitiello, Brad Smith," *CNNMoney*, July 18, 2012, http://tech.fortune.cnn.com/2012/07/18/new-business-models/.

[92] "Intuit Operating Values," Intuit, accessed July 2013, https://about.intuit.com/about_intuit/operating_values/.

[93] Roger L. Martin, "The Innovation Catalysts," *Harvard Business Review*, June 2011.

[94] Robert Cooper and Scott Edgett, "Ideation for Product Innovation: What are the best methods?", *PDMA Visions Magazine*, March 2008, http://www.stage-gate.net/downloads/working_papers/wp_29.pdf.

[95] Clayton M. Christensen, Scott Cook, and Taddy Hall, "What Customers Want from Your Products," Harvard Business School (Working Knowledge), January 16, 2006, http://hbswk.hbs.edu/item/5170.html.

[96] Horace Dediu, "Apple Stores Have Seventeen Times Better Performance Than the Average Retailer," Asymco, April 18, 2012, http://www.asymco.com/2012/04/18/apple-stores-have-seventeen-times-better-performance-than-the-average-retailer/.

[97] "Transcript: JC Penney CEO Ron Johnson," *CNNMoney*, July 18, 2012, http://tech.fortune.cnn.com/2012/07/18/transcript-ron-johnson/.

[98] Jackie Harper, "I Love Shopping at JCPenney (Don't Tell)," January 11, 2010, Free Is My Life (blog), http://www.freeismylife.com/2010/01/i-love-shopping-at-jcpenney-dont-tell.html.

[99] Danielle Sacks, "Ron Johnson's 5 Key Mistakes at JC Penney, in His Own Words," April 10, 2013, http://www.fastcompany.com/3008059/ron-johnsons-5-key-mistakes-jc-penney-his-own-words.

[100] Dale Furtwengler, "JCPenney: Not a Pricing Failure," *Pricing for Profit*, July 24, 2012, http://pricingforprofitbook.com/jcpenney-not-a-pricing-failure/.

[101] Stephanie Clifford and Catherine Rampell, "Sometimes, We Want Prices to Fool Us," *The New York Times*, April 13, 2013, http://www.nytimes.com/2013/04/14/business/for-penney-a-tough-lesson-in-shopper-psychology.html.

[102] Rachel Ehrenberg, "The Psychology of J.C. Penney: Why Shoppers Like It When Retailers Play Games with Prices," *ScienceNews*, April 22, 2013, http://www.sciencenews.org/view/generic/id/349890/description/The_psychology_of_JC_Penney_Why_shoppers_like_it_when_retailers_play_games_with_prices.

[103] Brad Stone and Jim Aley, "Amazon Doesn't Put Profit First," *San Francisco Chronicle*, January 19, 2013, http://www.sfgate.com/default/article/Amazon-doesn-t-put-profit-first-4208391.php.

Habit 5—Delight

[104] Matthew Dixon, Karen Freeman, and Nicholas Toman, "Stop Trying to Delight Your Customers," *Harvard Business Review*, July 2010.

[105] Timothy L. Keiningham, Douglas R. Pruden, and Terry G. Vavra, "The Role of Customer Delight in Achieving Loyal," Ipsos Loyalty (paper), June 2004.

[106] Recklessnutter, "Tesco Homeplus Virtual Subway Store in South Korea," YouTube, June 24, 2011, http://www.youtube.com/watch?v=fGaVFRzTTP4.

[107] "Customer Service Isn't Just a Department!", Zappos, accessed July 2013, http://about.zappos.com/.

[108] "Ryanair No 1 Customer Service Stats—January 2012," Ryanair, February 22, 2012, http://www.ryanair.com/en/news/ryanair-no-1-customer-service-stats-january-2012.

[109] "Ryanair Ranked 'Second Worst Short-Haul Carrier'," Budget Airline News, December 15, 2011, http://www.budgetairlineguide.com/news/184/ryanair-ranked-second-worst-short-haul-carrier/.

[110] Nate Schweber, "At La Guardia, a Smiling Helper Materializes, Digitally," *The New York Times*, August 8, 2012, http://www.nytimes.com/2012/08/09/nyregion/la-guardias-digital-avatar-gives-passengers-airport-information.html.

[111] Claire Cain Miller, "Starbucks and Square to Team Up," *The New York Times*, August 8, 2012, http://www.nytimes.com/2012/08/08/technology/starbucks-and-square-to-team-up.html.

Leadership

[112] Robert Nelson, "Sprint May Cancel Your Service If You Call Customer Service Too Often," TechnologyTell, July 6, 2007, http://www.technologytell.com/gadgets/26177/sprint-may-cancel-your-service-if-you-call-customer-service-to-often/.

[113] "Benchmarks by Industry: Wireless Telephone Service," The ACSI, accessed July 2013, http://www.theacsi.org/index.php?option=com_content&view=article&id=147&catid=14&Itemid=212&i=Wireless+Telephone+Service.

[114] Graham Hill, "Sprint Fires Its Unprofitable Customers," CustomerThink (blog), July 10, 2007, http://www.customerthink.com/blog/sprint_fires_its_unprofitable_customers.

[115] Barry Levine, "Sprint Nextel Cuts 4,000 Jobs, Closes 125 Stores," NewsFactor, January 18, 2008, http://www.newsfactor.com/story.xhtml?story_id=10200003IL0U.

[116] "Sprint Earns J.D. Power and Associates' Top Ranking—For Third Straight Time—for Purchase Experience Among Full-Service Wireless Carriers," August 9, 2012, Sprint (press release), http://newsroom.sprint.com/news-releases/sprint-earns-jd-power-and-associates-top-ranking-for-third-straight-time-for-purchase-experience-among-full-service-wireless-carriers.htm.

[117] Bob Thompson interview with Jerry Adriano of Sprint, "Sprint Answers the Call to Improve Customer Experience," CustomerThink (interview), July 22, 2010, http://www.customerthink.com/interview/jerry_adriano_sprint_customer_experience.

[118] Bob Thompson, "8 Big Ideas for #CX Success (highlights from Customer Experience Summit 2011)," CustomerThink (blog), November 10, 2011, http://www.customerthink.com/blog/customer_experience_summit_2011_8_big_ideas.

[119] Steve Lubetkin, "SNCR Podcast: Excellence in New Communications Award Winner Sprint Nextel Corp.," Society for New Communications Research, April 19, 2012, http//www.sncr.org/blog/sncr-podcast-excellence-in-new-communications-award-winner-sprint-nextel-corp.

[120] Christina Bonnington, "Report: Sprint Makes Multibillion Dollar Bet on the iPhone," *Wired*, October 3, 2011, http://www.wired.com/gadgetlab/2011/10/sprint-iphone-purchase-report/.

[121] Bob Hockman, "Network Performance Monitoring Critical for Smartphone User Loyalty," CustomerThink (article), June 20, 2011, http://www.customerthink.com/article/network_performance_monitoring_critical_for_smartphone_user_loyalty.

[122] Domenico Azzarello and Mark Kovak, "Can Communications Services Providers Earn Their Customers' Love?", Bain & Company (article), August 11, 2011, http://www.bain.com/publications/articles/can-communications-service-providers-earn-customers-love.aspx.

[123] Gerardo Dada, "Customer centricity as Sprint's turnaround strategy," Bazaarvoice (blog), July 6, 2010, http://blog.bazaarvoice.com/2010/07/06/customer-centricity-as-sprints-turnaround-strategy/.

[124] "2013 U.S. Wireless Network Quality Performance Study—Volume 2," J.D. Power (press release), August 29, 2013, http://www.jdpower.com/content/press-release/sP8rA2r/2013-u-s-wireless-network-quality-performance-study-volume-2.htm.

[125] Paul Hagen, "How Chief Customer Officers Orchestrate Experiences," Forrester Research (report), February 25, 2013.

[126] Jeanne Bliss, "CCO Structure & Team—Option 1: Staff Leader with a Dedicated Team," Chief Customer Officer 2.0 (blog), July 31, 2012, http://chiefcustomerofficer.customerbliss.com/2012/07/31/coo-structure-team-option-1-staff-leader-with-a-dedicated-team/.

[127] Bob Thompson interview with Jeanne Bliss, "Winning Back Customer Love, the Role of the Chief Customer Officer," CustomerThink (interview), May 16, 2012, http://www.customerthink.com/interview/chief_customer_officer_inside_scoop_with_jeanne_bliss_of_customerbliss.

[128] Bob Thompson, "Solving the 'Digital Experience Conundrum' for Large U.S. Banks," CustomerThink (blog), June 11, 2013, http://www.customerthink.com/blog/solving_the_digital_experience_conundrum_for_large_us_banks.

[129] Sonsofmaxwell, "United Breaks Guitars," YouTube, July 6, 2009, http://www.youtube.com/watch?v=5YGc4zOqozo.

About the Author

Bob Thompson is an international authority on customer-centric business management who has researched and shaped leading industry trends since 1998. He is founder and CEO of CustomerThink Corporation, an independent research and publishing firm, and founder and editor-in-chief of CustomerThink.com, the world's largest online community dedicated to helping business leaders develop and implement customer-centric business strategies.

Thompson is co-author of *The Blueprint to CRM Success* and author of the groundbreaking report "Customer Experience Management: A Winning Business Strategy for a Flat World." He has written numerous other materials on customer-centric business and is a popular keynote speaker at conferences and seminars worldwide.

Before starting his firm, Thompson worked in the IT industry for fifteen years. He held positions at IBM, where he advised companies on the strategic use of information technology to solve business problems and gain a competitive advantage.

27194396R00138

Made in the USA
San Bernardino, CA
09 December 2015